The HEROES Who Fell From Grace

The
HEROES
Who
Fell
From
Grace

The true story of Operation Lazarus,
the attempt to free American POWs
from Laos in 1982.

by
Charles J. Patterson
and
G. Lee Tippin
(Col. U.S. Army, Ret.)

Daring Books
Canton • Ohio

Published by Daring Books
P.O. Box 526 H, Canton, Ohio 44701

Printed in the United States of America.

This book is dedicated to the 2,497 American servicemen still missing in Southeast Asia;

And to.........
Their families who wait, hope, and pray;

And to.........
The four courageous men who tried:
> LTC James "Bo" Gritz
> Charles Patterson
> Gary Goldman
> Dominic Zappone

If it should be otherwise, if we should have to leave our bleached bones on these desert sands in vain, then beware of the anger of the Legions!

. . . Written by MARCUS FLAVINIUS, a Roman Centurian, over 2000 years ago.

LIST OF ILLUSTRATIONS

*Photograph in illustration insert sections

PREFACE

Their night-vision goggles made them look like visitors from outer space as they scanned the far bank of the mile-wide Mekong River, searching for signs of enemy activity. They stood there, four Americans in camouflage jungle fatigues, carrying UZI sub-machine guns and 150 pound rucksacks. Fifteen fierce looking Laotian anti-Communist guerrillas lounged nearby waiting for orders. Finally, the leader, a retired U.S. Army Special Forces colonel (who still wore a bracelet bearing the name of Robert Standerwick, an American pilot missing in action in Vietnam), tossed his rucksack over his shoulder and exclaimed, "It's a good night to die, fuck it. Let's go!"

And so, on 27 November 1982, a commando team of four Americans and 15 indigenous guerrillas, led by two former Green Beret heroes, James "Bo" Gritz (pronounced Gr-eye-tz) and Charles Patterson, climbed into three sampans in Thailand and launched a commando raid across the Mekong River into Communist controlled Laos. Their "mission impossible" was to liberate American POWs that intelligence sources said were being held in a prison camp near the town of Sepone, Laos—Americans who were still alive after more than 10 years in captivity; Americans who were officially listed as PKIA (Presumed Killed in Action) by President Carter; Americans who had been written off by their government; Americans who had been all but forgotten by the American people.

The fact that the operation was finally launched was, in itself, a minor victory for Bo Gritz. Against almost overwhelming odds, he had been struggling to mount a rescue mission for over three years. His crusade was launched in 1979 by certain high-ranking individuals in the intelligence community who were convinced that Americans were still being held in Southeast Asia and were dissatisfied with the administration's ineffective attempts to settle the question. Gritz had almost launched the rescue mission twice before, but each time it was scrubbed. From the very beginning he was plagued by a series of frustrations: off-and-on again quasi-governmental support, lack of funds, disgruntled and bickering team members, and major security leaks. An average man would have quit long ago, but Bo Gritz was not an ordinary man; he was a man driven; a man obsessed with one mission; a man who believed he was chosen by God "to rescue the American POWs still being held in Southeast Asia."

Patterson joined the rescue team in 1981. He and Gritz had been friends for many years, ever since the Vietnam War where they fought side-by-side in many battles. Their friendship had been forged in battle and tempered with blood and fire. Patterson thought of Gritz as a brother and so admired him that he had named his youngest son after the legendary SF officer.

The rescue mission ended in failure in a courtroom at Nakhon Phanom, Thailand, in February 1983. Gritz and his companions were given suspended sentences for "illegal possession of high-powered radio equipment." Patterson was not in the courtroom. The two comrades had become estranged during the operation; by the time of the trial, they were openly hostile.

Gritz returned to America amid a pandemonium of publicity and a press that welcomed him with open arms. As certain truths came to light, this romance with the media cooled quickly. The two combat veterans, who once had high hopes of rescuing fellow Americans from the hands of the Communists and who were willing to sacrifice everything to accomplish their mission, had suddenly become "The Heroes Who Fell From Grace."

When publisher Dennis Bartow (also former SF) of Daring Books phoned to ask if I would be interested in writing a book about *Operation Lazarus,* I admit I wasn't too keen on the idea. Like many Americans, I did not believe that there were American POWs still alive in Southeast Asia. I must confess I never thought much about it, perhaps because I wasn't directly affected. The war had been over officially for 11 years. Our POWs were repatriated in 1973—anyway that's what our government said. I could not see any logical reason for the Communists to continue to hold U.S. POWs. After a lifetime of soldiering, I am somewhat familiar with the machinations of the Communist mind. For their every act there is a reason; there must be a quantitative return for quantum effort. When I asked myself "why would the Vietnamese continue to hold American POWs?"", the only answers I could come up with were that (1) perhaps they wanted to embarrass the United States, or (2) that it satisfied their paranoia to foil the great superpower who was helpless to find an acceptable solution to the possibility that U.S. servicemen could still be living in captivity. Reluctantly, I agreed to meet with Charles Patterson, the second-in-command of *Operation Lazarus.*

Charles (Chuck) Patterson now lives in a small community in California with his wife Virginia and their children: Michael age 20; Lee Ann age 16; and Michelle age 12. He is presently working as a police detective in a small city nearby. In his spare time he raises and trains fierce German Rottweiler dogs to be used in police work. A native Californian, Patterson joined the Army in 1963, and spent 12 of the next 14 years in the U.S. Army Special Forces. He served two tours in Vietnam where he fought with the elite Green Beret Mobile Guerrilla Force (MGF) and the III Corps Mike Force (a Special Forces strike force made up of indigenous troops led by American Green Berets). He served two tours in Thailand, one with the JCRC (Joint Casualty Resolution Committee) seeking recovery of remains of U.S. servicemen missing in action (MIA). After the war he was assigned as an instructor at the U.S. Unconventional Warfare School at Fort Bragg, NC. He left the Army in 1977 after his young son was killed in a tragic shooting accident. He graduated from the California Police Academy, and for a time he worked as a deputy sheriff before becoming an undercover narcotics agent. His military awards and decorations include the Silver Star, two awards of the Bronze Star with "V" for Valor, two Purple Hearts, Army Commendation Medal, four awards of the Good Conduct Medal, the Vietnamese Cross of Gallantry, Combat Infantryman's Badge, Master Diver's Badge, Senior Parachutist's Wings, Vietnamese Parachutist's Wings, and Thai Parachutist's Wings.

Upon meeting Chuck Patterson one is immediately impressed by his size. He's not a giant, but he is big, heavily muscled, and a man of obvious physical strength; there is no doubt that he can take care of himself in a brawl. He exudes honesty and sincerity. It didn't take long to realize that Patterson believed—beyond a shadow of a doubt—that there still were captive Americans in Southeast Asia, that he joined the rescue operation because of a strong sense of loyalty and belief in its leader (retired LTC James "Bo" Gritz), and that he had an unselfish desire to help solve the POW question.

After hearing Patterson's story and examining the papers and documents in his possession, the POW/MIA question began to appear in a different light, lending credence to the possibility that:

— The Vietnamese and Laotian Communists could be withholding information regarding remains of U.S. servicemen.

— Circumstantial evidence indicated that there was a very real possibility that there are American POWs still being held in captivity in Southeast Asia.

Patterson's story should be written, letting blame for the failure of the rescue mission fall where it may. The adventure should be told to record how a group of courageous, dedicated ex-soldiers challenged overwhelming odds to attempt a mission that might save other American servicemen's lives.

Operation Lazarus was intended "to free at least one of the more than 2,494 Vietnam War American Prisoners of War or Missing in Action who were unaccounted for when Operation Homecoming (the return of POWs and remains agreed upon at the Paris Peace Talks) was completed in 1973."

After all these years, if there are live American POWs in Southeast Asia, what is their mental, physical and emotional condition? What do they think of their homeland for failing to rescue them? What if high-ranking members of the U.S. Government and the intelligence community knew that U.S. POWs might still be alive, and for some obscure political reason might have squelched such information? This would be a national shame of a gigantic magnitude!

This book has a diversified and complex cast of characters: The President of the United States, CIA and DIA agents, American generals and admirals, daughters of American MIAs, aging Laotian warlords, U.S. Congressmen, Laotian ex-Prime Ministers, Chinese Tong leaders, self-acclaimed assassins and soldiers of fortune, mercenaries and would-be mercenaries, guerrilla chiefs, secret agents from behind the bamboo curtain, actor Clint "Dirty Harry" Eastwood, Captain Kirk (actor William Shatner), billionaire H. Ross Perot, and former Green Berets and Navy SEALS.

In the final analysis, this is the story of two men, both genuine

American war heroes, who proved their mettle in combat during the Vietnam War. Retired Lieutenant Colonel James "Bo" Gritz was awarded more than 60 decorations, commanded the famous Green Beret Mobile Guerrilla Force, and survived numerous operations behind the enemy lines. Former Green Beret Staff Sergeant Charles J. Patterson was awarded over 20 decorations, fought as a member of Gritz's Mobile Guerrilla Force and later in the Indigenous Mike Force, and participated in many raids deep into enemy territory. This is their story as told by Chuck Patterson.

G. LEE TIPPIN

P.S. I regret that we had to omit several incidents from the story in the interest of national security; for the protection of certain indigenous personnel who are still operating behind Communist lines; and for fear of harassment and reprisal from certain individuals in our own government. (For example, when Gritz and Patterson returned from the mission, the IRS conducted a five-year audit of their tax records. Coincidence? Doubtful.)

ACKNOWLEDGEMENTS

The authors wish to thank Robert K. Brown, editor, and his personnel at *Soldier of Fortune* magazine: Jim Graves, Donna DuVall, Jim Coyne, and Alex McColl, for their assistance and contributions to this book. The authors freely used information and material that had taken these fine writers many long hours to authenticate and compile.

A special thanks to two close friends: Phyllis McClellan of Carmel, CA for her editorial assistance; and Gayle Osborn of Lockwood, CA for her aid and encouragement.

INTRODUCTION:
IF THEY ARE THERE

If the government of North Vietnam has difficulty explaining to you what happened to your brothers, your American POWs who have not returned, I can explain this quite clearly on the basis of my own experience in the Gulag Archipelgo. There is a law in the Archipelgo that those who have been treated most harshly and those who have withstood the most bravely, who are the most honest, the most courageous, the most unbending, never again come out into the world. They are never shown to the world because they will tell tales that the human mind can barely accept. Some of your returned POWs told you that they were tortured. This means that those who have remained were tortured even more, but did not yield an inch. These are your best people. These are your foremost heroes who, in solitary combat, have withstood the test. And today, unfortunately, they cannot take courage from your applause. They can't hear it from their solitary cells.

      ALEKSANDER I. SOLZHENITSYN, author
      of *THE GULAG ARCHIPELGO*

IF THEY ARE THERE, what is their mental and physical condition? How are they being treated? We know how they were treated.

NORTH VIETNAM MAY 1969

The guards hauled me off to what the POWs in the Zoo called the Ho Chi Minh room of the auditorium. I was dressed only in my black shorts and short sleeved shirt. By pulling on my handcuffed wrists, I was stretched out face down on a small table. The flailing began with what we called the "fanbelt." It was a strip of rubber cut from an old tire. The guards and prisoners used it as a rope to draw water out of the com-

pound's filthy wells. Once, when a piece broke off, a guard discovered it made a very effective whip.

In the Ho Chi Minh room, I began to whimper, then cry, then with each stroke scream. As the lashing continued, my screaming turned again into crying and, as the guards exhausted themselves, the crying to whimpering. I do not know how long it was before they stopped and dragged me to one of the office rooms where three interrogators waited. They were North Vietnamese I had never seen.

The game was about to start once more. To survive meant sticking to lessons already learned. The physical punishment had to be endured. But to keep it that last margin short of unendurable, I had to lie, delay, beg, try not to answer, confuse, even outwit them, if possible. But to make it all convincing I knew I must endure, I must endure, I must endure!

Although Ed and I agreed to answer questions about the escape, in the begining I refused to answer my questions. In the long run this was the best approach. Two guards grabbed my leg irons, jerked me off the stool, and dragged my butt across the rough red tile floor to face another interrogator. This was repeated a number of times. When one interrogator finished or hesitated in his questioning, two guards yanked on my leg irons and raced to the opposite side of the room where another interrogator waited. Soon I could feel the seat of my black shorts burning damp with blood.

If I confessed, my friend assured me the beatings would end and my tormentors would leave. Of course, as soon as an unacceptable answer was made, the beatings would start again. The brutal punishment continued without slacking. I could always tell when the camp commander was going to hit me. The guards would blindfold me first. His wallop was the hardest. I received steady attention from the Goose and "Vocal Cords", a methodic torturer who seemed pleased with his shabby job. The Goose was as emotional and excitable as when I had first been subjected to his talents two years earlier.

A routine developed. The Goose and Cords, who was constantly and loudly demanding something, would pull my *head back by the hair so that the other could steadily slap my face with the full leverage that comes from not having one hand tied up doing something else. Taking turns, they beat me about the face, then put me through the ropes.*

When my answers infuriated them, another beating followed. Each would start out slapping me with his right hand, then his left hand. When they realized they couldn't hit me hard enough with their left hands, they concentrated on getting more power out of their right-hand roundhouse swings. Soon their hands became fists. It was not long before the left side of my face was swollen and bleeding. My left eye was closed. A cloth was available to wipe the blood from their right hands.

They had developed some new variations of the rope ordeal. Initially, they had simply tied the rope to the wrist cuffs, thrown it forward over my shoulder, and threaded it down underneath the leg-iron and back up over the shoulder again. Then either Goose or Cords would plant a foot or knee between my shoulder blades. Goose was the more vicious. With that leverage, he would then pull on the rope with all his strength, trying to lift my arms up over my head. My screams accompanied his grunt.

Later to that excruciating ordeal they added a new twist. They would remove the handcuffs, position my arms in a double hammerlock, and tie my forearms and wrists together. With another rope they pulled my elbows in as tight as possible. Again they threw the rope forward over the shoulder then looped it under the irons and up again, as before. The jerk and then the steady pull increased tremendously the pressure on the tight double hammerlock. With a crafty smile, Cords attempted to assist the interrogators and please himself by anchoring the rope to my thumbs instead of to my wrists.

During those first five days, I was manacled the entire time by the leg-irons and hancuffs. At night, aided by a bright spotlight, the guards attempted to keep me awake, banging on the door shouting and coming in to slap my face if they thought I was asleep.

During the day, by plan or in uncontrolled agony, I cried, screamed, and begged them to stop.

LTC JOHN A. DRAMESI, USA,
former POW of the Vietnamese
in *CODE OF HONOR*, (W.W. Norton and Co., 1975)

Jane Fonda, where in the hell were you when we needed you?

There are still 2,497 Americans unaccounted for in Southeast Asia. Since the fall of Saigon, the Defense Intelligence Agency has received 1,682 reports concerning missing Americans in Southeast Asia. Of these, 327 reports were first-hand sightings of refugees. I believe the weight of the intelligence today proves that there are still American POWs being held against their will in Indochina.

LT GEN EUGENE T. TIGHE, JR.
Director, Defense Intelligence Agency
June 25, 1981.

CHAPTER ONE

CLARK AIR FORCE BASE, THE PHILIPPINES, 12 FEBRUARY 1973.

Millions of Americans sat, eyes glued to their televisions, watching the historic drama unfold. Operation Homecoming (the return of POWs and remains agreed upon at the Paris Peace Talks) was about to begin. The C-141 Starlifter transport taxied slowly to the parking ramp, shuddered, and settled. The engines softly cried to a stop. Uniformed attendants rolled the debarking steps into position. A red carpet was unrolled from the bottom step to the roped-off waiting crowd.

The door of the Starlifter opened outward and a gaunt man dressed in Navy khaki appeared on the steps, his hand raised in greeting, his face alight with unashamed happiness. Captain Jeremiah Denton, U.S. Navy, the first American off the plane, descended the ramp and stationed himself before the waiting microphone, and—in a moment the nation will long remember—said, "God Bless America!"

Around the world, millions of throats constricted with emotion as people watched the homecoming through moist eyes. The returnees spurned the iced-tea served on the two-hour flight and clamored for beer. They were oblivious to the "brass" in the reception line urging them to pause for a photo with high-ranking officers. They disregarded the roped aisle to waiting buses to scurry them to Clark Air Force Base for thorough physicals. The returnees ducked under ropes, sprinted to the wildly cheering crowds that lined the runway, hugged and kissed the ladies and slapped men on the back. At the hospital, they partied 24 hours, refusing to stay confined to assigned rooms, sent broth back to the kitchen demanding steak, and depleted stores of ice cream and milkshakes. Any physical problem caused by years of malnutrition, torture and abuse could wait until all five senses assured them that this was, in fact, the good old God Bless America U.S. of A.

America breathed a big sigh of relief; the long, agonizing ordeal of the Vietnam War was over. The unpopular war had torn the very guts out of our nation and American youths burned draft cards and fled the country rather than serve. The Vietnam War caused Americans to march in the streets in protests and at least one popular movie star espoused the enemy cause. It was high time to put our country back together and put the terrible ordeal behind. Despite accounts of barbaric tortures our prisoners received at the hands of their Communist captors, it was time to forget if not forgive. Peace with honor had been achieved. The American prisoners were coming home. Altogether, 116 men were airlifted that day from Gia Lam Airport. During the next five days, a total of 591 Americans returned. A happy America echoed "God Bless America" and closed its eyes, minds, and hearts on the longest and most psychologically devastating war in U.S. history.

This stirring scene should have marked the end of the anguish and the beginning of happy times, but it did not. There were still 2,497 American servicemen unaccounted for in Southeast Asia. For the families of those still missing, it certainly was not the end. What about the missing? How many were still alive? If they were dead, where were their bodies? If they were alive, why didn't the Communists return them as agreed in the Peace Treaty? Were they holding them for bargaining chips at some future negotiating table? Were they holding them because they were maimed and disfigured? (It is a fact that not one of the returnees was maimed or disfigured.) Were the Communists surprised because we didn't demand an accounting? Was our administration more interested in "normalizing" future relations with Vietnam than in demanding a full accounting of our POWs and MIAs? In an effort to get the war over quickly and expeditiously, did our administration "write them off?"

Almost immediately, the U.S. Government found itself suppressing information that Americans were alive and still being held by the Vietnamese. On 11 June 1973, a classified cable was sent from the American Embassy, in Saigon, to the Secretary of State. The subject was an NVA (North Vietnamese Army) rallier/ defector who was surfaced by the Saigon government and made available to the media. The defector brought news of six American servicemen still held by the North. The cable continues, ". . . requested news services to play down details."

By 1974, the rumblings of abandoned Americans were echoing through the halls of Congress, producing an intercepted Senate document stating, "The administration must ask itself what price it should be willing to pay for such limited returns." "Limited returns" referred to American POWs and MIAs.

By mid-1975, throngs of refugees began pouring out of Vietnam, Laos, and Cambodia. With them came a myriad of reported sightings which fell on deaf ears. These refugees were not, as a matter of policy, being questioned regarding Americans being held.

In 1977, President Carter appointed the Presidential Commission on American Missing and Unaccounted for in Southeast Asia. The Commission was briefed by the CIA (Central Intelligence Agency), DIA (Defense Intelligence Agency), and the JCRC (Joint Casualty Resolution Center). Armed with 150 folders containing detailed information of locations where missing servicemen had gone down, the Commission flew to Hanoi. They were wined and dined by the Communists, but only one folder was presented to the Hanoi government. The Commission concluded that improved relations between the two countries held out the best hope for a full accounting.

Military men who accompanied the Commission said they were ashamed to be Americans. "The Commission was an embarrassment to us." Former Deputy Assistant Secretary of Defense Roger Shields said, "The Commission was intended to make the Vietnamese look cooperative and thus bury the issue." Congressman Robert K. Dornan, of California, said, "The Vietnamese made fools of them."

Shortly after the Commission's return to America, Carter or-

4

dered a case-by-case status review of American MIAs. (Just two months earlier, he had promised the League of Families of American POWs and MIAs, that he would not do this.) Those unaccounted for were labeled PKIA (Presumed Killed in Action). Carter now had what he wanted. The door was open for the Vietnamese application to join the United Nations to go unchallenged by the United States.

★   ★   ★

CALIFORNIA, USA, AUGUST 1981

"Slow down, honey. You're driving too fast."

Chuck Patterson glanced down at his speedometer. The indicator was pushing 70. He was excited and anxious at the prospect of seeing his old friend and Vietnam commander, but his wife was right. It wouldn't be good for a police officer to get a speeding ticket. He eased up on the accelerator, and the blue Olds settled back to an acceptable 60 mph. His wife, Virginia, relaxed in the passenger seat.

Patterson hadn't seen Bo Gritz since 1971. It had been a shocking surprise to learn that his old boss and comrade had retired from the Army and was living in Los Angeles. Like most who knew the legendary Green Beret officer, Patterson always figured that Bo would stay in the service and someday make general. He was finally able to get Gritz's phone number from a friend and call him. When Gritz invited him to LA for the weekend, it was tantamount to an order.

Patterson admired Bo Gritz more than any man alive. Their friendship had been solidly forged on the field of battle in blood, steel, and death. There is no comradeship closer than that of men who have lived together through the ultimate adventure of war; and, only those who have graduated with honors can understand this bond—"The Brotherhood of War."

★   ★   ★

While attending high school at Fort Union Military Academy in Virginia, Gritz had seen a poster that changed his life forever. It

RESUME
James "Bo" Gritz

JUNE 1981

IMMEDIATE
CAREER OBJECTIVE

Liberate US POWs held by the Communists in
Southeast Asia.

SPECIAL QUALIFICATIONS

o Special Forces Command and Staff Officer with
24 years experience planning and conducting
special operations. Expert in use of weapons,
demolitions, communications, and first aid.
o Fluent in Chinese Mandarin, 77 weeks intensive
training at the Defense Language Institute.
o Chief of Congressional Relations, Office of the
Secretary of Defense, DSAA, two years.
o Public Affairs Assistant to the Secretary of the
Army and Army Chief of Staff.
o Foreign Area Specialist, Asia, Africa, Latin
America.

CIVIL/MILITARY
EDUCATION

o PhD Candidate, Psychology, Roosevelt University
o MA, Communications, The American University
o Military Science, US Army Command & General
Staff College (Honor Graduate)
o BS, Law Enforcement & Corrections, University
of Nebraska
o Certified/Registered Hypnotherapist
o Certificate, Swahili and Chinese Mandarin.

SPECIAL SKILLS

o Commercial pilot and Certified Flight and Ground
Instructor, multi-engine, instrument (3,000 hours)
o Sixth Degree Blackbelt, Tae Kwon Do Karate;
Chief Instructor, American Council on Karate
Instruction
o Lockmaster: Key and Safe lock manipulation;
security systems. Space Shuttle Security Design.
o Underwater Demolition and Salvage Diver (Army)
o Master Parachutist, Conventional and High Altitude
Low Opening, 750 jumps.
o Army Ranger, Pathfinder, Combat Infantryman.
o Army Special Forces Instructor, Special Warfare
School, Unconventional/Guerrilla Warfare, Air &
Amphibious Operations

AWARDS & ACCOMPLISHMENTS

o More than 60 awards & decorations for heroism
and achievement including: 3 Silver Stars,
2 Legion of Merit, Distinguished Flying Cross,
Soldier's Medal, 8 Bronze Stars "V", 26 Air
Medals "V", 4 Army Commendations "V", 2 Purple
Hearts, Presidential Citation, Numerous Foreign
Awards including 7 Cross of Gallantry and Gold
Medal of Cambodia.

Figure 3

read—*The U.S. Army Special Forces are the world's toughest troopers.* The primary mission of the Special Forces (SF) was to infiltrate deep behind enemy lines and organize and train guerrilla units to attack enemy lines of communication. It was a challenge the young man could not resist, so after graduation he joined the Army and was accepted into the elite Special Forces. His primary specialty became demolitions, but he also trained in communications, first aid, sabotage, small unit tactics, hand-to-hand combat, intelligence gathering, and weapons (both U.S. and foreign). A few months later he attended Officer's Candidate School (OCS) and was commissioned a Second Lieutenant of Infantry. Already a paratrooper, he soon graduated from the Army's tough and physically demanding Ranger School. James "Bo" Gritz was ready to go to war.

He went to war in 1963, where he soon became a legend in the Special Forces. He commanded the Mobile Guerrilla Force (MGF) which had the mission to search out and destroy the enemy. He led raids deep behind the Communist lines, and, in the process, his men killed hundreds of enemy soldiers. (There are estimates that say Gritz was responsible for killing over 650 Communists.)

In his book on the Vietnam War, *A Soldier Reports,* General Westmoreland describes Gritz as "the daring young commander of one of the first mobile South Vietnamese guerrilla forces to be organized." He goes on to describe how Gritz recovered a highly secret "black box" that the Viet Cong had taken from a downed U-2 spyplane. Gritz spent four tours in Vietnam and accumulated a chest full of medals. He became one of America's most decorated soldiers, an accepted expert in special operations, and a professional highly respected by his fellow Green Berets.

The green and white highway sign read "Los Angeles 28 miles." Patterson glanced over at his wife. Evidently more comfortable with his slower driving, she had dozed off. Yes, he had known Bo for many years. He reflected and smiled to himself as he recalled their first meeting. It was February 1967, and Patterson had just arrived in Vietnam assigned to Company A, 1st Special Forces in Bien Hoa, as a demolition specialist. He was walking across the compound to the mess hall when, suddenly, the quiet day was broken by the familiar "thrump, thrump" of rotor blades. Four helicopters swooped in and settled on the Landing Zone (LZ) amidst swirling dust. A group of ragtag soldiers jumped from the choppers and came strolling across the field. They wore tiger suits (special camouflage fatigues), bush hats, and red-white-and-blue scarves. Their uniforms were torn and caked with mud, and, in some cases, blood. Some of the soldiers were wearing field dressings. It was clear that they had just come from battle. The few Americans dispersed among the group had several days' growth of beards. All in all, they looked like a "bad-assed" bunch of troops.

Patterson instantly knew who they were. Everybody in the Special Forces knew about the famous Mobile Guerrilla Force. The unit was composed of Cambodian and Nung mercenaries, led by American officers and noncommissioned officers (NCOs). Their mission contained only three words: Search and Destroy. Their job was simple: find the enemy and kill him. Only the very best Green Berets were selected for the MGF. It was the elite of the elite.

Patterson decided then and there that this was the outfit for him. He had come to Vietnam to fight. He was anxious to get out into the boonies and mix it up with Charlie (slang for Viet Cong). He stopped one of the weary looking Americans. "Hey, who does a guy see about getting into this outfit?"

The Green Beret Sergeant never broke stride; he gestured over to one of the parked helicopters, "That Captain standing over there."

Patterson looked at the man pointed out to him. There was no way to tell whether or not the soldier was an officer; he wasn't wearing any rank insignia. Patterson walked up and saluted, "Sir, I'm Specialist Patterson and I'd like to get out into the jungle and fight with your unit."

Tilting back his bush hat, Captain Gritz rested his Swedish K submachine gun on his right shoulder. His steel blue eyes held Patterson's. "Can you fight?"

"Yes Sir, I can!"

"If you get into this outfit, the only thing I can promise you is a damn good body bag if you are killed, or a damn good party if you live through an operation."

"Sounds fair enough to me," returned Patterson, trying his best to sound brave.

"Okay, meet me down at the Kol Lok Bar tonight and I'll see if you can fight. If you can whip five gawd damned *legs* (slang for soldiers who are not airborne qualified), then I'll get you into my unit."

That night Patterson walked into the Kol Lok Bar (local Vietnamese Officer's Club). As usual, the Club was packed with off-duty American Military Policemen. The Vietnamese whores were busily plying their trade. Every once in awhile a soldier would disappear behind the curtains where there were a series of small rooms, which were more like horse stalls than rooms. It was here that the "business ladies" would take it upon themselves to make a little money. It wasn't very romantic, but it was an easy, cheap, and quick way of getting your "ashes hauled."

The MGF leader was seated at a table with two Green Beret sergeants. Patterson joined them and ordered a beer. Gritz didn't at first acknowledge the newcomer, then finally he looked across the table. "Well, your time's on. You have to whip five of these sons-a-bitches or you're not fit for this team."

Patterson figured—it's now or never! He took a deep swig of beer and pushed his chair back. He stood up and looked around the room. His eyes settled on the biggest SOB in the bar. He walked over to his target and, without a word of warning, he hit the man with a round-house right. The "leg" fell backward as if he had been pole-axed and lay still on the floor. The fight was on; every MP in the place wanted a piece of him. Patterson had stirred up a nest of mad hornets.

The young Green Beret felt a grazing blow to the side of his head and turned to face his next adversary. He swung from the belt and floored his second leg. A solid smash to his mouth sent him reeling back against Gritz's table. Patterson glanced down to see the young Special Forces Captain casually chatting with the men seated with him, seemingly oblivious to the fight going on around him. Patterson realized he sure-as-hell was not going to get any help from his fellow Green Berets. Gritz looked up and held up two fingers. Boosting himself away from the table, Patterson shoved back into the melee. After about 15 minutes, the job applicant had three men out, a fourth stretched across a table, belly up, and the fifth braced against the wall signaling enough.

Patterson made his way back to Gritz's table. His lips were cut and blood dribbled down his chin. Bo finished his drink, pushed his chair back, and stood up. "Report to work at 0600 tomorrow. I'll fix it with the Sergeant Major and Colonel."

Without another word, Gritz walked out of the bar.

*In June 1980, a Vietnamese mortician,
hooded to protect his identity, testified before
the House Subcommittee on Asian and Pacific
Affairs. The mortician, an ethnic Chinese
expelled from Vietnam due to his lineage,
claimed that as late as 1977, he had personally
processed the skeletal remains of 426 Americans
currently being stored at 17 Ly Nam De Street,
Hanoi (known to American POWs as "The
Plantation") adding he had witnessed live
Americans in detention. The DIA verified the
allegations via independent sources and gave
the mortician a polygraph test—which he
passed.*

UNITED STATES DEFENSE
INTELLIGENCE AGENCY

CHAPTER TWO

Patterson pulled up in front of the modest Gritz home in the Westchester suburbs of Los Angeles. He and his wife were greeted at the door by a smiling, ageless Gritz. The two men shook hands; Bo's grip was like steel. It was obvious that he was still in good physical condition for there wasn't an ounce of fat on his lean, muscular body. He was wearing a blue T-shirt and light blue slacks. On his bulging left bicep, a bald eagle fluttered each time he moved his hand. Bo still looked every inch the professional soldier that he was. Patterson, who recently had acquired a few extra pounds, felt himself automatically drawing his stomach in. As he entered the house, the ex-sergeant noticed a sign on the door: "POWs Never Have A Nice Day."

Bo's wife, Claudia, entered the room, and introductions were made. The last time the Pattersons had seen Bo, he was married to Cary, his third wife, a lovely Chinese lady he met while serving in Vietnam. Claudia, herself a raven-haired beauty, was obviously much younger than her husband; but after a few minutes, Patterson could see that she was very devoted to Bo.

Gritz didn't offer any booze because he had quit drinking several years ago. They all seated themselves in the small living room, and Claudia poured coffee. The room was moderately decorated, but Bo's presence was reflected. Over the mantle above the fireplace was a framed certificate from the American Council on Karate Instruction, which had awarded Bo its highest honor, a sixth-degree black belt.

Gritz started the conversation. "So, how do you like being a policeman, Pat?"

"It's great, but I'd still rather be back in the Army. I guess what I'd like most would be to get a Warrant Officer Commission and get into the Army CID (Criminal Investigation Division)."

"Pat, why did you get out? I figured you for a lifer."

"It's a long story, but I'll try and make it short. I guess nothing was the same after Nam—the Army just went to hell!"

Gritz picked up, "Yeah, that's true. Things weren't the same for me either. I began to feel like a dinosaur—obsolete. The challenge and excitement were gone."

Patterson took a sip of his coffee, set his cup on the table and continued, "Then, some shit-head in Washington said I had to get out of Special Forces for awhile and get my ticket punched. So they sent me to DI (Drill Instructor) School and then to Fort Ord to push basic trainees. You talk about a crappy job; I hated it from the beginning. We were just a bunch of damned nursemaids. We had to tuck them in at night, and pat-em-on-the-ass and graduate them. Training was pitiful; we sure as hell weren't teaching them to fight. I was getting fed up with the whole system. Then one day Jimmy got into my closet and found my revolver. It fell on the ground and discharged. He died several hours later. It was a freak accident because the damned thing had a trigger guard locked on it. After that, I guess I went sort of crazy. The world closed in on me. Things at work went from bad to worse. I was afraid that I would lose my temper and beat the shit out of some trainee, or worse, kill him . . . so I got out. Now, I wish to hell I'd had the right kind of help and weathered it out. I regret my decision . . . but it's too late to cry over spilt milk."

Gritz knew about the tragic death of his namesake, but he couldn't find words to comfort his friend. What the hell can you say about something like that? Both men were warriors and had seen men die in combat; both had killed many times. But something like this—a young boy playing with his father's gun! What pain, guilt and self-recrimination Patterson surely felt; what anguish he must have gone through! What can be said? Bo decided it was time to change the subject. "Come on out to my office, I want to talk to you. The wives can gossip about us."

Gritz led him out the back door to a small building next to the garage. His office was filled with that memorabilia only a professional soldier accumulates in a lifetime of soldiering. The walls were covered with plaques from the various units in which he served. There were framed certificates from the schools he had attended: Ranger, Airborne, Pathfinder, Demolition, Scuba, Locksmith, Defense Language Institute (he speaks fluent Chinese), Command and General Staff College, and even hypnotism. The center of attraction was a glass case displaying most of his sixty-plus military awards and decorations.

Gritz touched his cup to Patterson's. "To the good old days; and to those we left behind."

"I miss the good old days," returned Patterson.

Bo sat down at his desk and motioned Patterson to a nearby chair. "How would you like to go back to the good old days?"

"Sometimes I wish I could. Those were the best days of my life. I shouldn't say this but I enjoyed the hell out of Vietnam. I felt alive and useful—and challenged. I haven't had the same feelings since."

Gritz's next words were, "I'm going back. I have a job to do, and you're welcome to come along."

Patterson looked at his old commander, questioningly. "What do you mean by that?"

"What if I told you there were live American POWs still being held in Laos and I've been asked by the government to launch a rescue mission?"

Patterson was startled. He had never known Gritz to lie, but this was bizarre! He could see by Gritz's eyes that the legendary Green Beret was not joking. "I-I've heard stories about live POWs, but I just thought they were a bunch of crap. If there were any, our government would have done something by now."

Gritz looked up from the desk and smiled. "Oh, would it?" He opened the center drawer and withdrew an 8 × 10 inch black and white photograph and pushed it across to Patterson. "Here, take a close look at that! A certain Congressman, who shall go unnamed, dubbed this photo 'Fort Apache'."

The Special Forces NCO picked up the picture. It clearly showed a compound with hooches (huts) and four guard towers. In the center of the camp was a group of men in a formation. The compound was surrounded by rice paddies. Patterson's trained eyes recognized the typical Southeast Asia prison camp.

"That picture was taken over Laos by a Big Bird satellite just seven months ago!" announced Gritz. "Take a close look at those men in the center of the camp. Their shadows are longer than the men standing in a circle around them. A DIA photo analyst identified them as Caucasians!"

Patterson's heart jumped into his mouth! He couldn't believe what he was seeing. 1981? American Prisoners of War? Photo taken over Laos? By a satellite? For Patterson, like most Americans, the war had been pushed deep into his memory. The whole idea of live Americans in Laotian prison camps was totally unthinkable, but the proof was in his hands!

Gritz pointed to a spot on the photo with a pencil. There, as clear as day, was the number 52. Patterson knew it was common practice during the Vietnam war for American POWs to mark the location of their prison camps by the number 52. It identified their presence and precluded random bombing by U.S. aircraft. And here at Fort Apache, after having been prisoners for nine years or possibly longer, 30 Americans had not given up hope. They were still holding out, keeping the faith, believing that sooner or later someone would come for them and the "52" was there for just that reason.

"Holy shit!" exclaimed Patterson, "Why hasn't the government done something?"

"Why? I'll tell you why. Because certain people high up in the government would be embarrassed. This photo isn't all; I have a stack of classified DIA documents six inches thick that prove the existence of American POWs at other locations. Officially, Washington has kissed-off this photo as Russian advisors, but that's a bunch of bullshit!" He tapped the photo vigorously with his index finger, "These are Americans, by damn, I'm going to bring them out! Sometimes I think that only God, the mothers, and the Special Forces want the prisoners out. The entire POW/MIA issue opens

15

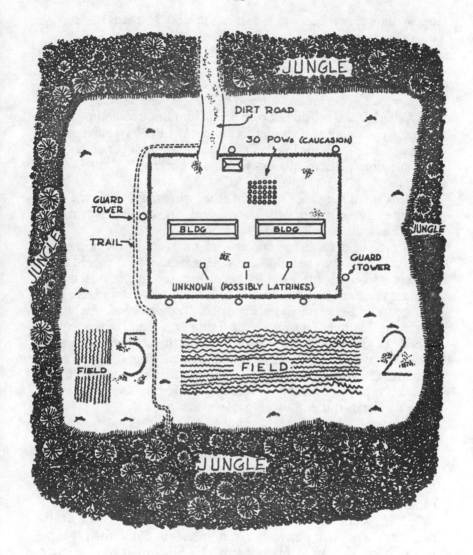

Figure 5
Fort Apache (as remembered by Chuck Patterson).
The actual photograph was taken at an angle.

up wounds of war that nine years has healed. It seems like no one in America wants to get embroiled in that war again."

"I don't understand. You said earlier that the government gave you the mission. Now you say they have officially declared the photo as not being Americans. So how can you mount an operation without full government support?"

"Well, thank God, there are a few influential people in government that do want to do something about the POWs. I have certain contacts; that's where I've been getting the intelligence data. So I'm not alone; I have quasi-government backing."

"Quasi?"

"Yeah, quasi," smiled Gritz. "In other words, if we fail, the sons-of-bitches never heard of us. They would just say, 'It was crazy old Bo Gritz and his Over-the-Hill gang.'"

Gritz paused for a moment to let his words sink home. He wanted Pat on this operation. He needed someone he could trust, someone who wouldn't desert him when things got rough. The combat veteran SF Sergeant was fearless in combat and one helluva good soldier, but, more important, he was loyal. Pat would never quit on him. During *Velvet Hammer,* several of the experienced special operations veterans had quit, mostly because he couldn't pay them. Hell, he hadn't taken a cent out of the kitty for himself. Claudia was working at Hughes just so they could pay their bills. He had quickly lost all respect for those who quit. He hadn't promised them a rose garden.

Patterson's adrenalin was pumping. He didn't have any reason to doubt Bo's words. Bo was closer to him than his own brother. He had bet his life more than once on Bo Gritz. What Bo said was always gospel. He would never lie to him. Patterson could see the fire in Bo's eyes when he spoke, and he had seen that before, in combat.

"Three years ago," said Gritz, "I was asked to get out of the Army and organize a private rescue mission. Since then, I have run into roadblocks at every turn. The first mission, *Operation Velvet Hammer,* was well on the way when I had to scrap it in April because of official pressure and lack of funds. But, right now I have a new charter for the mission. At this very moment, we have two indigenous patrols in Laos, reconnoitering Fort Apache. Ben Dunakoskie, J.D. Bath, Scott Barnes and Vinnie Arnone are in

Thailand waiting to debrief the patrols. They should be back by the first of December, and I hope to launch the rescue mission shortly after that."

AUTHOR'S NOTE: How Scott Barnes ever became part of Gritz's operation, only God and Bo Gritz will ever know. Barnes is a genuine 10 carat flake, habitual liar, fraud, and all-around world champion weirdo. He makes great personal claims to have worked for the CIA as an assassin; to have headed a super-secret POW rescue team; to have been in the Green Berets and the Navy SEALS; and to have been once sent to Laos to kill two captured CIA agents who were caught by the Communists while they were in Laos "planting yellow rain." His most memorable lie was his claim to writer Alan Dawson of the *Bangkok Post* "that he swam acros the Thai-Cambodian border to look for POWs." If he did, then he is the first and only man in recorded history to accomplish such a feat, because there is no water there! It is a land border.

"I know Dunakoskie and J.D. Bath," said Patterson. "They are both good men, but I don't know Barnes and Arnone. What are their backgrounds?"

"Vinnie was in Nam with the Forces; he's a character, but he's a good troop. I don't know much about Barnes. He came to me and said he was a friend of General Vang Pao and wanted to help on the rescue mission. He claims to be former Special Forces, but I haven't had a chance to check him out yet."

It wasn't like Bo to send a man on a mission without checking him out first, thought Patterson. Maybe old Bo was slipping a little.

Gritz stood up and put his hand on Patterson's shoulder. "Pat, I need you on this operation. I want you to be my executive officer. And this time, by gawd, we're going to make it. I'm tired of fucking around! I know that it is my destiny to rescue the prisoners. God has chosen me for this task. The only thing that can stop us is if the government arrests us for conspiracy to violate the U.S. Neutrality Act; but I don't think anyone is going to try." Gritz paused and his steel-blue eyes blazed at his friend, "Are you with me?"

Bo needed him! Patterson didn't hesitate for an instant. "Damn right I'm with you! All the way!"

"Good! We were always one hell-of-a-team. This time we'll make history. Now, let me tell you how I got involved in this thing and what has happened up to now."

*Anyone who fought and gave his blood in
that country still has emotional ties there. I still
have a hollow place in my heart ever since.
Nixon said we got out with honor. That's
bullshit! There is no withdrawal with honor. A
warrior comes home on his shield or carrying it.
We did neither. We basically bugged out of
Vietnam, and we did it without resolving the
case of our own people. We'll have gotten out
with honor when we can account for all of our
MIAs and POWs.*

LTC JAMES "BO" GRITZ,
U.S. Army (retired)

CHAPTER THREE

OPERATION VELVET HAMMER

In 1976, LTC Gritz was commanding the Special Forces Battalion
in the Panama Canal Zone. The mission of his unit was to provide
unconventional warfare support to Latin America and to help
defend the Panama Canal. One of his major activities was sending
small mobile training teams to Central and South American nations to train the indigenous forces in guerrilla and unconventional warfare. For a peacetime mission, it was a good command
with enough classified operations to make it interesting.

General Harold R. Aaron, the Army's Chief of Intelligence, visited Bo's battalion in August. Aaron had once commanded the
Special Forces in Vietnam and for a time was Gritz's boss. After
the formal briefing, General Aaron took Gritz aside and informed
him that "there was increasing evidence that there may still be
some American prisoners held by the Communists in Southeast
Asia." Later in the conversation he implied that the Executive
Branch did not consider it politically expedient to pursue the
matter, and were, in fact, "squelching" the evidence, but he didn't
say why. He asked Gritz to start thinking of ways to confirm the
fact that American POWs might still be alive.

The Green Beret colonel was shocked by the General's statement: first, by the admission that there were live Americans and, secondly, that the President's office was writing them off.

A few months later, Gritz was transferred to Washington to serve as Chief of Congressional Relations of the Defense Security Assistance Agency. He suspected that General Aaron was behind the transfer.

In October 1978, General Aaron (then Deputy Director of the DIA) again approached Gritz. He told the young officer that overwhelming evidence had been accumulated that American POWs were alive and being held by the Communists in Southeast Asia (SEA) and that the Carter administration was politically handcuffing the intelligence community. "For them," he said, "the problems did not exist. Therefore, there is only one way to handle the situation. We would like you to consider retirement so that we can arrange for you to accomplish, through the private sector, what uniformed intelligence is prevented from doing."

AUTHOR'S NOTE: General Aaron is now dead and Gritz's claim that the General asked him to retire and organize a rescue mission cannot be verified.

Gritz interpreted the General's request as an order. He promptly submitted his retirement papers. To those that knew him it came as quite a shock. Even the *Army Times* made a comment about his premature retirement.

A cover job was arranged for Gritz in the Overseas Operations Department of Hughes Aircraft Corp. in Los Angeles. He was allowed "no questions asked" travel to defense installations in the U.S. and overseas.

Gritz had no more than settled into his new office when he received a phone call from Texas. It was H. Ross Perot, the multibillionaire electronics magnate. Perot spoke short and to the point. "This is H. Ross Perot. I want you to come to Dallas to see me today."

Perot's spacious office was situated on the top floor of a ten-story building, surrounded by a private 18 hole golf course, all covered by a tight security complex. When Gritz stepped out of the elevator, he was met by retired Green Beret Colonel Arthur "Bull" Simons. Colonel Simons, himself a legendary soldier and well-known expert in special operations, led the raid on the Son Tay POW camp near Hanoi in 1970 and engineered the rescue of two of Perot's employees from Khoumeni's Iran in 1980.

Simons spoke first. "Bo, I'm getting too old to execute this type of mission, so, I'm going to plan it, you're going to execute it. You've got a history of being hard-headed, so I must know one thing: Are you going to be able to work for me?"

"Sir," returned Gritz, "I'm hard-headed when I'm dealing with staff-pukes that try to tell me what to do when I don't think they know what they're talking about. But I respect you, and I'll carry out any order you give—you can count on it."

Simons nodded his head and ushered Gritz into Perot's office. Perot, a graduate of the Naval Academy, is a man proud of his personal discipline and military training, and runs his empire like a military organization. He wasted no time, and came straight to the point. He told Gritz that General Eugene F. Tighe, Jr. (Director of the Defense Intelligence Agency) had asked him to look into the POW/MIA situation from the private sector and that the General wanted to use Gritz as the "action man." Perot asked Gritz to go to Southeast Asia and look into the situation, but added, "I don't care about bones. I wouldn't pay one cent for a bone!"

Gritz finally had his marching orders, straight from the Director of the DIA through Ross Perot! If he found evidence of live POWs and a positive identification of a location, Bull Simons would plan the raid, and he would command the ground operation. The entire operation would be financed through the private sector under the direction of H. Ross Perot.

AUTHOR'S NOTE: When H. Ross Perot was questioned about Gritz's story, Perot said, "He came to me, explained his plan, and I told him I didn't think it had a chance of working and that he should go directly to someone in the government." Perot denies that Gritz went to Asia at his request, and he said he only met with Gritz once and that meeting was at the request of Ann Mills Griffiths, Executive Director of the National League of POW/MIA Families.

A spokesman for Perot, William Wright, acknowledged that his boss met once with Gritz. He said that Perot paid Gritz $922.50 to defray the cost of Gritz's flight to Texas.

During the next three months, Gritz traveled throughout Southeast Asia gathering evidence and questioning eye-witnesses. He interviewed dozens of official and unofficial sources: contacts from his four years in Vietnam, free Laotian guerrillas, Vietnamese resistance forces, refugees, boat people, and other U.S. intelligence sources.

One Vietnamese who had been a political officer in the Saigon government told Bo that three groups of Americans remained in Vietnam: former POWs who had married Vietnamese women and who were permitted a modest degree of freedom; deserters or turncoats (this group was believed to number 12); and prisoners of war unacknowledged by the Communist Government. This latter group was spread out in small groups throughout Laos and Vietnam.

The DIA added more input to Gritz's growing pile of evidence. They interviewed a former Vietnamese Colonel, Ngo Van Trieu, who resided in Paris. Ngo Van Trieu claimed to have observed a total of 28 Americans at a camp near the Cambodian-Vietnamese border. He said that most of them wore black and white striped uniforms and were very thin. They moved slowly and listlessly and looked very tired.

Finally, Gritz interviewed a refugee who had escaped from a Vietnamese prison camp in August 1978. The refugee claimed he had been held with 49 Americans. The refugee's daily task was to clean the American's individual hooches. He gave the location and described the camp in detail. He even offered to accompany an American rescue force.

As the retired U.S. Army colonel gathered evidence, he began to see several reasons for the Communists to continue to hold U.S. captives. First, Americans captured in Laos and Cambodia fell into a separate category from those captured in Vietnam. The United States had vehemently denied that we ever conducted war in these two countries. Therefore, if U.S. servicemen were captured in a country which was a noncombatant area, then technically they were not prisoners of war. In the eyes of the Communists, these men would be labeled criminals and not eligible for repatriation. (It is a fact that no live U.S. POWs have ever been returned from Laos and Cambodia.)

Second, it is contrary to Communist practice to give up potential political assets without some sort of compensation. Twenty-five years after the French Indochina War (1954), the French Government was still negotiating on a case-by-case basis for the remains of its soldiers; not one body has been returned free-of-charge.

And third, President Nixon and Secretary of State Henry Kissinger, hastening to conclude a war that was tearing away the very soul of American society, secretly promised the Communists some $3.25 billion in economic aid. This money was never approved by a hostile U.S. Congress. Not trusting American promises, the Vietnamese held American POWs to use later as bargaining chips.

AUTHOR'S NOTE: The Vietnamese say they are not obligated to provide an accounting for U.S. POW/MIAs because the U.S. did not live up to its obligation to provide reconstruction aid to the Socialist Republic of Vietnam. According to the Vietnamese, President Nixon promised in a letter to Premier Pham Van Dong, dated 1 February 1973, to "unconditionally" provide reconstruction aid to Vietnam in the amount of $3.25 billion. Both Nixon and Kissinger deny that the letter was part of the 1973 Paris Peace Accord. They claim the purpose of the letter was to outline what the U.S. could do to help Vietnam, within the Constitution, and that it was not intended as an unconditional promise of aid.

The Nixon/Pham Dong letter and the nature of the American commitment, if any, to supply the reconstruction aid specified in the letter continues to be an unresolved issue. The pertinent portions of the letter follows (The italics are the Author's):

The President wishes to inform the Democratic Republic of Vietnam of the principles which will govern United States participation in the postwar reconstruction of North Vietnam. As indicated in Article 21 of the Agreement on Ending the War and Restoring Peace in Vietnam, signed on January 27, 1973, the United States undertakes this

participation in accordance with its traditional policies. These principles are as follows:

1. The Government of the United States *will contribute to postwar construction in North Vietnam without any political conditions.*

2. Preliminary United States studies indicate that the appropriate programs for the United States contribution to postwar reconstruction will fall in the range of *$3.25 billion* of grant aid over five years. Other forms of aid will be agreed upon between the two parties. This estimate is subject to revision and to detailed discussion between the government of the United States and the government of the Republic of Vietnam.

ADDENDA

Understanding Regarding Economic Reconstruction Program:

It is understood that the recommendations of the Joint Economic Commission in the President's note to the Prime Minister will be implemented by each member in *accordance with its own constitutional provisions.*

NIXON etc. etc. . . . .

It is clear from the text of the letter that President Nixon did indeed promise the money to North Vietnam. It is also clear to see why the Communists are angered by this broken promise.

★   ★   ★

While Gritz was overseas, Colonel Simons died while undergoing open heart surgery. America lost one of its finest warriors, and Bo lost a creditable advocate in court.

Perot agreed to go on with the POW efforts provided that the refugee (the one who had escaped from a Vietnamese prison camp in 1978, and had agreed to go back with a U.S. rescue force) could be polygraphed and verified as telling the truth.

The DIA decided that it would be best if the refugee could be brought to America to take the polygraph test. So, on 10 August, General Tighe wrote a memorandum to the Secretary of Defense. The subject was the prompt entry into the United States of a Vietnamese refugee who had reported American prisoners of war in Vietnam as late as 1978:

> *A Vietnam refugee (name deleted) who is presently in a refugee camp in Indonesia has reported that from December 1977, through July 1978, he was with 49 Americans. If the substance of information is true, then its importance goes without saying . . . I feel there is an obligation on the U.S. Government to make every effort to confirm or deny this report and this can best be done through interrogating him in this country. Recommend you sign the enclosed letter requesting Mr. Vance's assistance in this matter.*

One week later, 17 August, the Secretary of Defense forwarded the request to the Secretary of State:

> *Dear Cy,*
> *I have received a report of a Vietnamese refugee in Indonesia who claims to have been detained in the northern part of Vietnam with forty-nine American prisoners of war, as late as July 1978. Could you help?*
> *Sincerely, Harold.*

One month and one day later, 18 September, Cyrus Vance replied to Harold Brown's request:

> *Dear Harold,*
> *In view of the decision of the Immigration and Naturalization Service not to admit this individual into the United States you might wish to consider approaching the Commissioner of Immigration to have the decision changed.*
> *Sincerely, Cy.*

The refugee was never admitted to the United States and his tales, true or false, disappeared with him. According to Gritz, H. Ross Perot withdrew his support at this time.

AUTHOR'S NOTE: H. Ross Perot denied that he had any knowledge of these efforts by Gritz. General Tighe admitted that he knew Perot but denied having any POW dealings with him.

Every year, one to two million illegal immigrants enter the U.S. It seems that if the government were serious about solving the POW/MIA issue, someone in a position of authority would have "pulled the necessary strings" to get this one refugee admitted into the country. This memorandum-shuffling episode is a prime example of "passing the buck" and a red tape bureaucratic Washington runaround in which no one had the "guts" to make a decision. Surely, the almighty Secretary of State has some influence with the Commissioner of Immigration.

★   ★   ★

Gritz returned to Southeast Asia to continue investigating POW sightings. In October 1979, the French newspaper, *Le Martin,* published an interview with Mister Le Dinh, a former North Vietnamese intelligence agent who had defected to the West. Le Dinh admitted that "some of the more stubborn American prisoners had not been exchanged in 1973."

By the end of 1980, Gritz was becoming increasingly frustrated. He had been concentrating on the POW/MIA Project for two years and had compiled mounds of circumstantial evidence. He was convinced that Americans remained alive in SEA and the more we delayed in rescuing them, that many more prisoners might die. He was "champing at the bit," yet the launch date for an operation was no closer than it was two years ago. He felt like he was getting the old Washington bureaucratic run-around; and he was beginning to realize that there were VIPs (very important people) in the government that did not want to address the POW/MIA problem.

In April 1980, one of General Vang Pao's patrols stumbled across a "POW Detention Center" in Eastern Laos. General Vang Pao's forces fought the Communists in Laos during the war. After the war, the CIA gave Vang Pao a barley ranch near Missoula, Montana, for "services rendered." The old General still controls several hundred H'Mong resistance fighters in Northern Laos. It is his people, the H'Mong, who are being exterminated by the Communists with the deadly "yellow rain." Vang Pao's patrol returned to Thailand to report having seen "30 Americans" being held by the Communists. The sighting was passed on to Vang Pao, in America, who in turn forwarded it to the CIA. Bo would never find out why a reconnaissance flight was not flown immediately; but something happened in Washington's bureaucratic maze. It was eight months later, in January, that the satellite snapped the picture of Fort Apache—the same photograph that Gritz showed Patterson in August 1981.

It now seemed apparent to the American intelligence community that there was indeed overwhelming evidence that American POWs were still being held in SEA. However, there were still those who didn't want to open old wounds. Gritz was called back to Washington and, finally, with the financial backing of a front company named "Agronomics," Bo was given the go-ahead for his mission, by certain unidentified members of the intelligence community. He gave the impending operation the code-name *Velvet Hammer*. (*Velvet Hammer* was designed as a blow to the Vietnamese, but a cushioned blow that would not humiliate them and thereby endanger the lives of other prisoners in other camps.)

Given the green light, Gritz charged ahead. He began visiting military installations and R&D (Research and Development) laboratories, searching for the latest developments in weapons, communications, and special equipment. He located several items that he believed would be useful on the rescue mission:

-- AR-180: A light-weight, silent automatic machine gun with a laser light sight mounted beneath the barrel. The laser pinpoints the target and the strike of the bullet is "zeroed" to the laser spot. The weapon is capable of cutting a car in half.

-- Probe-Eye: an infrared optical system that discriminates between human and animal forms and between armed and unarmed people in the dark.

-- Inflatoplane: A rubber airplane that can be parachuted to the earth in a 55-gallon drum. The craft weighs only 250 pounds with its hand-cranked drone engine. It carries one passenger besides the pilot. (At one time Gritz considered "surgically" freeing one POW and flying him back to free territory using the Inflatoplane.)

AUTHOR'S NOTE: The AR-180 has not lived up to expectations; the rim-fire cartridge tends to jam after a few rounds and the scope and battery gives the weapon a gross weight of over 22 pounds. Several Police SWAT Teams purchased the weapon and, in most cases, it ended up collecting dust in their arms rooms.

We still have French prisoners! They were not fit to return to their families so we never released them. Don't you want to see your family again? There are still Frenchmen in our prisons who did not reform their minds. We can keep you forever!

(These words were spoken by North Vietnamese interrogators to several American POWs during their captivity.)

JOHN G. HUBBELL
in *POW.*

CHAPTER FOUR

Through the "Special Forces Old Boy Network", Gritz put the word out for volunteers. *"Bo Gritz needs a few good men for a secret commando raid into Communist Laos to rescue American POWs."* Special Forces combat veterans are a special breed of man —a blood brotherhood. Most of these veterans have friends who disappeared during cross-border or classified operations. Gritz felt that his call to arms was a challenge no true Green Beret vet could turn down. The fact that he—one of the most decorated and respected officers in the Special Forces—was going to command the rescue attempt was thought to be a special incentive. There was also a psychological appeal because most Americans who fought in Vietnam still think that we left work undone over there. Last, but not least, there is the "Last Hurrah Syndrome" that many old soldiers have—the opportunity to participate in one last battle, one last good firefight! Once it enters, the smell of cordite never leaves a man's system.

On 1 March 1981, 26 men answering Gritz's call assembled at the American Cheerleader's Academy at Leesburg, Florida. Bo's second-in-command was retired Sergeant Major Tommy Tomlin, who had a distinguished record with special operations in Vietnam. Medal of Honor recipient, Fred Zabitosky, Son Tay raider Earl Bleacher, and Special Forces veterans J.D. Bath and Jim Donahue all gave up good paying jobs to join Gritz. James Monaghan and Tom Smith, two more SF veterans, walked away from newly established, profitable businesses. Gordon Wilson, ex-SF and ex-CIA operative, was selected to be comptroller. Sgt. Major Warren "Po" Pochinski, who spoke fluent Vietnamese and had served with Gritz in Panama, was the interpreter. Another former Green Beret, Harry Holt, was selected for his tactical planning abilities. Terry Smith, a six-foot seven-inch giant, who served as a member of SOG (Studies and Observation Group), a highly secret unit that operated behind enemy lines, was appointed physical training (PT) instructor. Others that responded to Gritz's call included Dick Hebert, a retired Marines Corps pilot and Lieutenant Colonel, and Mark Berent, a retired Air Force fighter pilot and Lieutenant Colonel (both of whom had flown many combat missions in SEA), Mike Reynolds, Tom Zineroff, Dominic Zappone, Butch Jones (Gritz's brother-in-law), Eric Anderson, Tom Cook, Bobby Stewart, Fred Leenhouts, Dave Ryder, and Bob Owens. Herbert and Berent were direct links to Fred Smith, President of Federal Express, a major potential financial backer for the project.

Gritz's Washington contact informed him that President-elect Reagan had been briefed on the proposed operation on 15 January, and was enthusiastic over the prospect of the rescue mission. While unable to express an open commitment, Reagan promised moral support and no interference.

When training commenced, Gritz added several other people to his team: Ann Mills Griffiths from the National League of POW/MIA Families; Gil Boyne, a hypnotherapist; Karen Page, a psychic from Los Angeles; and two reporters, Barbara Newman from *ABC* and Art Harris of the *Washington Post*. Both reporters agreed to maintain secrecy until receiving Bo's permission to release the story.

AUTHOR'S NOTE: With the exception of Ann Mills Griffiths, who had a personal interest in the operation, the other newcomers' presence should have sounded a warning to even the bravest of clandestine operators. The first day of training involved physical training at 5:30 a.m., followed by a mission briefing by Griffiths. She and several of the experienced SF veterans were concerned about the presence of the media. Said one veteran, "We had all been under the impression that this was supposed to be a co-

vert operation; as far as I was concerned, after participating in numerous covert operations, the cover for this operation was blown at this time."

Gritz explained that the reporters were there at his request because he wanted an accurate record of the operation and that he didn't worry about security leaks because the reporters knew that physical reprisals would be taken against anyone who compromised the mission.

Gordon Wilson put it in plainer words: "If anybody compromises this operation with premature publication of a story about it, they will be dead. We'll kill them!"

Another SF veteran said, "To invite the press in to observe the preparation for a covert operation was the most stupid damned thing I ever saw!"

The psychic, Karen Page, got up and told the team that she had been having visions for a long time about a camp in an unidentified country. "There is a house and beneath the house there are cells or doors, and on the doors are metal chains with little tags hanging on them—something of a dogtag type of thing."

During the next week Gritz's commandos took PT twice a day, spent the day planning the operation and received mass hypnosis every evening from Gil Boyne. The purpose of this exercise was to program them for the upcoming mission.

Gritz told his men that the operation wouldn't take long because "we have to get back as soon as possible because of the victory parade that we'll have down Fifth Avenue."

He discussed the parade several times and talked about how "we are going to sell the book rights and movie rights to Hollywood." He frequently held church services and expounded in his sermons on their role as "great saviors with God on their side." He claimed that he was "ordained by God to accomplish this mission, and his team were his disciples."

It was during one of these sessions that Barbara Newman decided that she had seen and heard all she could take, so she left the camp shaking her head to clear the fog.

During one psychic session, Bo began talking about two of the team members, saying he suspected they were CIA agents infiltrated into the operation to sabotage it. Karen Page immediately held a seance and claimed to be seeing a building in Washington, "No, in Virginia", with a sign saying "CIA" on it.

On one occasion, Gritz announced that everyone would be issued cyanide capsules so as to avoid capture and torture. They would take their own lives. He expected everyone to comply and even discussed "wiring it to our teeth so that we'd just bite down on it."

Bill Horan, the owner of the Cheerleading Academy, arranged for a friend of his, a reporter from the Leesburg newspaper, to have a personal interview with Gritz. A reporter from the *Orlando Sentinal* came along. According to Gordon Wilson and Gritz they extracted a promise, under "threat of death," that the reporters would not release the story before the operation.

By this time, Earl Bleacher, Fred Zabitosky, Jim Monaghan, Tom Cook, and Tom Smith had left the operation because of the "unprofessional methods" of its leader. Gritz claimed that they couldn't pass his training program and were dismissed.

Gritz divided *Velvet Hammer* into six phases:

Phase 1. Preparation and planning.

Phase 2. Training and familiarization with equipment.

Phase 3. Movement to Thailand.

Phase 4. Launching of the mission and liberation of the prisoners. The tentative attack date was set as 16 April 1981.

Phase 5. Extraction of the rescued prisoners from Laos to a safe location. Heading the list would have been "Jolly Green Giants" (Sikorsky CH-53 helicopters capable of airlifting 50 people). If air support from the U.S. Government was denied, there would be an overland exfiltration. POWs not healthy enough to move on their own would either be left in a safe area (area controlled by anti-Communist forces) or photographed and left behind.

Phase 6. Demobilization of both the American and Laotian guerrillas.

★   ★   ★

On 18 March, Gritz received gut-shattering news! He was informed that President Reagan had decided, after being fully convinced that there were U.S. POWs in SEA, that the U.S. Government forces would conduct an officially sanctioned rescue mission. The JSOC (Joint Special Operations Command) at Fort Bragg was to develop the plan for the mission. The Delta Force (the government's supersecret anti-terrorist strike force) was to conduct the operation. These were the same units that had planned and carried out the unsuccessful attempt to free the American hostages in Iran. Gritz was skeptical; he believed that the same thing might happen on this mission. The military had only six weeks to plan, prepare, and launch the raid before the monsoon season set in. He didn't think they could do it. The government plan called for launching their airborne assault from the South China Sea flying across Vietnam into Laos. They would have to have good weather to have any chance for success.

On 26 March, the story of *Operation Velvet Hammer* appeared as the front page headline of the *Orlando Sentinal Star*. So much for good security. *Operation Velvet Hammer* was finished as far as being a covert operation.

AUTHOR'S NOTE: On 30 March, the day President Reagan was shot, Gritz sent a memorandum (see page 34) to the President and other top administration officials in which he revealed the existence of the private rescue mission and requested that it be allowed to "parallel" any official effort to rescue the POWs.

The memo was hand-delivered to Washington and given to National Security Advisor Richard V. Allen. Allen was furious to find out that a private rescue effort had progressed so far without his knowledge and that Gritz had been given access to classified DIA intelligence information.

Gritz claimed that he wrote the memo because the only

MEMORANDUM FOR RECORD

TO: PRESIDENT REAGAN

THROUGH: SECRETARY HAIG

            SECRETARY WEINBERGER

INFO: NATIONAL SECURITY COUNCIL

SUBJECT: Liberation of U.S. POW's from Laos

REFERENCE: Ongoing military option involving JCS; Delta Force, Ft. Bragg,
            N.C. JUWTF/JSOC

PREFACE: The United States intelligence community is aware of the fol-
            lowing concept and the classified data contained therein upon
            which it is based. However, in light of the immediate sens-
            itivity of this plan and recent activation of military assets,
            it is imperative to bring this concept directly to the atten-
            tion of the President and his immediate advisors. Why? We have
            reason to be acutely concerned about the real danger that
            those aware of this option will not be inclined to present
            such a daring proposal to the highest levels of decision-
            making before it becomes too late to consider or exercise as
            a viable option.
            From Lt. Col. James C. (B.) Gritz (Army retired)
                 URGENT AND EXTREMELY CONFIDENTIAL

                    CONTAINS DIA INFORMATION
                    CLASSIFIED TOP SECRET

Handwritten note: Cover to letter to President outlining Velvet Hammer

Figure 6
*Cover letter for Gritz's Memorandum
to the President. Note the TOP SECRET
classification at the bottom of the letter.*

way top officials in the administration could be made aware of the private option was for him to tell them. "There is no way people who had fed me intelligence could inform their bosses about a totally unauthorized operation."

On 24 April, Gritz flew to Washington and vainly tried to get the charter for the rescue mission turned back to his unit. He met with Rear Admiral Jerry O. Tuttle, then Deputy Director for Intelligence at the Defense Intelligence Agency and the man who had headed up DIA's POW task force since October 1979. The Admiral was sympathetic but said the official mission had progressed too far to halt. He asked Gritz to consider returning to active duty and help plan the official effort.

AUTHOR'S NOTE: Admiral Tuttle admitted meeting with Gritz. "He's been involved in this stuff for two years and I wanted to tap his expertise. He may have been thinking about a private rescue mission, but I wasn't."

Lieutenant General Phillip Gast, Operations Officer for the Iranian mission and chief planner for the proposed SEA rescue mission, did not want Gritz back in the Army to help plan the raid—the General and Bo shared little love for each other.

On 20 May, Gritz received a phone call from his contact in Washington. He was informed that the next day's *Washington Post* would feature a story saying that patrols had been sent into Laos seeking U.S. POWs and none were found. The official rescue mission—the Delta operation—was cancelled. Bo did some checking and found that one of the patrols was sent to Atta Po, which was a way-station some 30 miles from the Fort Apache location; whereas, the second patrol was detected before it went 40 miles into Laos and was forced to turn back. Then the weather window slammed shut as the monsoon season arrived. He figured the government took the easy way out and cancelled the operation with the lame excuse, "No evidence of U.S. POWs was found."

"Had they kicked me and my men loose, 30 Americans might have been home, or at the very least, no longer abandoned into the hands of their enemies. Both they and the world would have known America cared."

★   ★   ★

AUTHOR'S NOTE: Perhaps the most damning aspect of *Operation Velvet Hammer* is that reputable, combat-experienced veterans, such as Earl Bleacher, Fred Zabitosky, Jim Monaghan, and Tommy Tomlin became disillusioned and quit the operation. Even Ann Griffiths from the National League of POW/MIA Families bailed out.

These people gave several reasons for quitting: First, they believed that there was a total lack of security because of the presence of the news media. Second, the money promised them, $7,000, was never paid. They didn't expect to get rich, but they believed that they needed enough for their families to live on while they were with the operation. As it turned out, 20 men had to borrow money—just to get home. Third, there was no proven viable target and no viable plan for getting the rescue team and freed POWs out of Laos. Fourth, there was some question whether the U.S. Government was backing the operation. How do you define quasi-backing anyway? Finally, the religious rhetoric and church services held by Gritz were considered "radical" by most of the team members. "I'm not agnostic," said one, "but this was a bit too much for me, especially the joining hands and singing hymns, so I walked out."

Alex McColl writing in a special Spring issue of *Soldier of Fortune (SOF)* magazine summarized the reasons for the failure of *Operation Velvet Hammer.* In the opinion of *SOF,* and in the opinion of several of the participants, *Velvet Hammer* was killed by a combination of factors, any one of which would have resulted in the failure of the mission:

1. *Lack of Funds.* There was never enough money on hand to run the project. One of the serious complaints against Gritz is that he asked people to quit paying jobs

and scuttle profitable businesses to go on a mission for which he did not have the resources to complete.

2. *Lack of Intelligence Information.* No one at the training camp actually saw the now legendary Fort Apache photograph. There was never any hard, detailed, reliable intelligence on which to base the mission.

3. *Lack of Security.* The media were fully briefed on everything from day one.

4. *Lack of a Plan.* There was never a viable plan to move weapons, radios, and other sensitive items to Thailand. There never was a viable plan to extract the team and any POWs that might be released after the target was hit.

5. *Lack of Government Sanction.* The men on the operation were told that Gritz had "tacit approval" of the U.S. Government, but it appears that only Gritz knew for sure.

6. *Lack of Professional Leadership.* Gritz was heavy on "bumper sticker rhetoric" and vague generalities, but was thoroughly lacking when it came to giving detailed planning and professional decision-making.

SUBJECT: News Media Release

FORUM : New York Vietnam Veteran of the Year Award, Buffalo, NY, 29 May 81, 12:00 noon.

FROM : James "Bo" Gritz, LTCOL US Army, ert; Commander, <u>Project</u> Velvet Hammer. Operation to Liberate US POWs in SEA.

POINT : You should read and consider using the attached information in your news reports.

REASON : There is good reason to believe the government is dumping an operation to liberate US POWs in Southeast Asia because it may be more trouble than it's worth to Washington bueaurcrates.

EXAMPLE: For two years I have been in close contact with Pentagon officials while developing confirmation that US servicemen are being held against their will by the Communists in Vietnam, Laos, and Cambodia. Since January 28, 1981, the National Security Council has known about a target containing POWs. My own private operation was asked to stand down so that the USG could pick up the action. I was told by a key official, "I have them (the Administration) by the balls and they can't turn around on this one." I was further told that our private plan had a better chance of success, but the President was excited about the rescue and would not release the operation back to us. I was invited back into uniform so that I might help the JCS plan and execute the rescue. Suddenly it is all off.

SUMMARY: Sudden disclosure by the Pentagon that their efforts to confirm US POWs failed might appear convincing to an uninformed public, but to those of us who have been working the inside, it is a clear cover-up and cop-out. If US POWs were rescued it would leave egg on the face of many politicians and government officials who have taken the 'leave well enough alone' attitude. All POW/MIAs have been declared "DEAD" leading families to spend money sent home and saved for the servicemen. Wives have remarried. It would cause an administrative enema within the Pentagon. Prior to our stand down the Pentagon assured us that our timeframe would be maintained. Our launch was planned so that we would be on target and out before the monsoon began in May. Delays carried the Pentagon plan until now it would be risky to conduct. Bad weather degrades communications, makes low level flying difficult and prevents over-flight photography. I think the Pentagon fooled around until it was too late and realizing that private sector was monitoring their progress, decided to abort. Our POWs are still there waiting for rescue and we should not allow the government to stand down even though it might be opening Pandora's Box to press-on.

I'LL WAGER THE TWO MEN WHO KNOW MOST ABOUT THE EXISTANCE OF US POWS, ADMIRAL TUTTLE AND GENERAL TIGHE (DIA) WILL BOTH BE MOVED ON TO OTHER ASSIGNMENTS NOW THE CAT IS OUT OF THE BAG. AND NEW OFFICERS PUT IN THEIR PLACE WHO DON'T HAVE A HOLD on sensitive parts of the political anatomy.

Figure 7
News release prepared by Gritz after
Operation Velvet Hammer was called off.

*Navy Commander Ronald Dodge was shot
down over North Vietnam on 17 May 1967.
Eyewitnesses saw him bail out and land. Dodge
then radioed his wing man. "Here they come;
I'm destroying my radio." That same day a
Vietnamese radio transmission was intercepted
that declared they'd caught the bandit pilot.
Later that year, a photograph of Dodge
surrounded by Vietnamese guards and civilians
was featured in the French magazine, Paris
Match and on the cover of Life magazine. The
North Vietnamese denied that they had him.
When the list of POWs came out, Ron Dodge's
name was not there. In 1981, eight years after
the war, the Vietnamese turned the bones of
Commander Dodge over to the U.S.
Government!*

CHAPTER FIVE

OPERATION GRAND EAGLE

In June 1981, Gritz received a telephone call from an intelligence
agent who called himself by the code name "Shipman." The agent
asked for a meeting with Bo concerning the cancellation of *Velvet
Hammer*. After a James Bond routine of changing cars and hotels,
Shipman finally introduced himself as part of a "super-secret organization created by the President to handle such activities as *Velvet Hammer*." Shipman told Gritz that his "Activity" (Intelligence
Support Activity or ISA) would soon be given the charter to conduct POW rescue missions. He asked Bo to be their principal
agent. Gritz would be allowed to select and lead his own men and
all funding would be supplied by the Activity. Gritz had known
Shipman several years before when the agent was in the Special
Forces. From there Shipman had joined the Defense Intelligence
Agency—Gritz suspected that Shipman was still with DIA and
attached to the Activity.

The new operation was code-named *Grand Eagle*. In private,
Gritz always referred to it as "BOHICA" (Bend Over Here It

Comes Again). Gritz was having serious doubts about the government's sincerity concerning the POW/MIA issue. He had a premonition that *Grand Eagle* was just another smoke screen.

★   ★   ★

A new plan was prepared in July—this time involving General Vang Pao's forces. The ex-Laotian General flew in from his Montana ranch and met with Gritz and Shipman in Congressman Robert Dornan's office in Los Angeles. The Congressman, who was not present, was Chairman of the Congressional Task Force on the POW/MIA issue.

A number of paramilitary groups have tried to secure Vang Pao's assistance in activities across the border in Laos. However, the General had always refused and remained loyal to the U.S. Central Intelligence Agency. When he found out that Vang Pao wanted to meet with him and discuss POWs in Laos, Gritz was surprised. He had avoided any contact with Vang Pao because he believed the General was a political-minded egotist who was only interested in becoming rich and famous.

Much to Gritz's surprise, Vang Pao was loaded with information about Pathet Lao and Vietnamese prison camps. The General named locations, numbers and dates that he could only have known if he was the one who passed it on to the government, which he claimed he did. According to Vang Pao, he had passed the information to U.S. intelligence sources in April 1980, but nothing happened, and he was angry with the government because it did not react positively to his reports. He claimed that he wanted nothing more to do with the U.S. Government. He asked Gritz if he was still on active duty, or acting as an agent of the government. Gritz assured him that he was a private citizen and working strictly through the civil sector. The rapport between the two soldiers grew and before the meeting was over they made an agreement. "Vang Pao would locate U.S. POWs still in Laos through his guerrilla and underground apparatus. Gritz would provide the where-with-all to liberate them, using U.S. commando volunteers, special equipment, and Vang Pao's paramilitary organization as support." They established a target date of October, 1981. This coincided with the seasonal intensification of Red Chi-

nese activities across the North Vietnamese border. Vang Pao said
that this would pull most of the Vietnamese forces away from the
target area.

Gritz immediately sent a team of four Americans (Bath,
Dunakoskie, Barnes and Arnone) to Thailand to work with Vang
Pao's forces. Their main job was to debrief the patrols upon their
return from Laos.

SEPTEMBER 1981

Patterson returned to Tehachapi and quit his job. Two weeks
later he was back in Los Angeles working with Gritz on *Operation
Grand Eagle*. At first, his wife was furious with him for joining the
venture—even threatening to get a divorce; but finally she accepted the inevitable. She knew that he felt very strongly about
the rescue mission; and her husband's loyalty and faith in Gritz
was something she couldn't fight. Chuck had not been the same
since the untimely death of their son, and he was obviously un-
happy away from the Army—maybe this operation would help
him regain his perspective. "Go ahead," she said reluctantly. "Get
it out of your system. Only be careful and don't get killed. I've
gotten kinda' used to having you around."

Patterson immediately began a program to get into shape. Each
day, he ran several miles, lifted weights and bicycled for one hour.
He knew what lay ahead because he had done it before in Vietnam. They were going to have to walk several hundred miles,
carrying heavy rucksacks and weapons; and there might be times
when they would have to run or even fight. Combat is the most
physically demanding activity in the world, and if you aren't in
good shape, you won't survive very long. His wife chided, "You're
too old and out of shape to do this sort of thing!" But he figured her
wrong. Hell! He could still outwalk any twenty year old! Besides, as
a police officer, he had stayed in pretty good shape.

As the days went by, Patterson began to feel alive again. He was
being rejuvenated by a purpose and a challenge. He had a reason

for living again. And it was like old times to be working with his charismatic friend.

Gritz was now in everyday contact with the chief of the secret Activity, code named "Cranston." Patterson never met either of Gritz's contact men, Shipman and Cranston, but he did talk to them on the telephone. Just based upon conversations with them and Gritz, Patterson had the distinct impression that Daniel Johnson[1], alias Shipman, was with the Defense Intelligence Agency; and Jerry Koenig[2], alias Cranston, was with the Central Intelligence Agency; and they were working together on the joint Activity.

★   ★   ★

27 AUGUST 1981

Gritz and Patterson met with General Vang Pao, this time in Garden Grove, California, at one of the General's United Lao Development Offices. Vang Pao mentioned that Bo's strange friend had come to visit him before their last meeting but he had forgotten to mention it.

"Which friend are you talking about, General?" asked Gritz.

"Why, Mr. Scott Barnes, of course."

"But he came to me and said he was your friend and was working with you," returned Gritz, beginning to smell a rat.

"Oh no! I only talked to him because he was your friend. I think we have a dishonest man in our midst."

"Well, he's over in Thailand now with the rest of my team. Don't worry. I'll take care of Mr. Barnes."

Patterson's first instinct had been correct. Bo had committed a security violation and now the team was infiltrated. He just didn't know who or what with!

Vang Pao shrugged his shoulders. "I will let you handle it." Then he went on to tell them that 90 percent of the Lao people support a unified front without Vietnamese. He believed that if Gritz and his men could liberate U.S. POWs, it would do three things: First, it would bring world attention to focus on the problems in Laos and

---

[1, 2] Names changed to protect identity.

the Vietnamese presence. Secondly, it would begin action through the United Nations to stop Soviet-backed chemical attacks on the H'Mong tribesmen. The Communists had been trying for years to exterminate the H'Mong who were loyal to the U.S. during the war. Vang Pao's men had brought back samples of the chemicals used, but by the time they got to analysis facilities in the U.S., the chemicals were inert and no identification had been made. Third, Vang Pao saw himself someday taking over the reins of government in Laos.

At the end of the meeting, Vang Pao handed Gritz a letter of introduction, written in Thai, to give to his main contact in Thailand:

HAVE RECEIVED BOTH YOUR LETTERS AND UNDERSTAND THE TEXT. I AM EXTREMELY PROUD TO RECEIVE NEWS FROM YOU ON OUR LIBERATION UNITS.

BELOVED, WITH THIS I AM WRITING TO DEPEND UPON YOU TO HELP THE ?????? THE AMERICANS SAY THAT THE GROUP DELIVERING THIS LETTER TO HELP LOOK FOR OUR SOLDIERS, THE GROUP THAT KNOWS THE LOCATION OF THE PRISON HOLDING AMERICAN PILOTS STILL ALIVE IN KHAMMOUANE. THAT'S THE NHEMORRATH AREA FOR THE MOKTHING AREA OR THE NORTH VIETNAM-LAOS BORDER.

TAKE A GROUP AND SEARCH AND DRAFT A PLAN TO BRING THEM OUT. IF WE CAN GET TWO AMERICAN PILOTS STILL ALIVE WE GET ANY SUPPORT IN THE AREA OF LIBERATING THE NATION.

THEREFORE REQUEST YOU HELP TO MAKE CONTACTS TO LOOK FOR ANYONE WHO KNOWS OF THIS MATTER. ALSO PLEASE HELP.

FROM PHAYE NARAPANOK
GENERAL VANG PAO

★   ★   ★

Vang Pao's patrols returned a month late. The last one closed into Thailand in late November. The intelligence received indicated that his troops had located four camps where Americans were still being held. "Some of the Americans were wearing shirts marked with the letters 'TB' for Tu Binh—Prisoner of War in Vietnamese." On the 21st of November, Gritz sent a message to the Americans in Thailand directing them to launch two Laotian patrols to reconnoiter and photograph the four potential targets. The Laotians were given NIKON F-3 cameras (purchased by Gritz), taught how to use them and sent back into Laos.

During the last week of November, Gritz, Patterson, Harry Holt, and Walter "Butch" Jones met with Congressman Robert Dornan in Los Angeles. An ex-pilot himself and a Korean War Ace, Dornan had some strong feelings on the POW/MIA issue. For one thing, he firmly believed that there were still Americans being held in Southeast Asia. One of his close friends, Air Force Colonel David Hrdlicka, was shot down over Northern Laos on 18 May 1965. A Chinese news agency quoted Lao spokesmen admitting they had him. The following year the Pathet Lao broadcast a letter from Hrdlicka to his wife. And in 1966, the Moscow *Pravda* published a clear photograph of the Colonel as an enemy captive. Yet after all of this, the Communists now claimed they never heard of him. He had just disappeared in Laos, like the "man who never was."

"It is absolutely sickening to think that an American could suffer such a fate," declared Congressman Dornan in public testimony in 1980. "I just can't conceive of what an American must think of his country if he is still alive somewhere in one of those jungle camps!"

Gritz arranged the meeting with Dornan because he believed he was still getting the bureaucratic run-around from Washington. He felt that a few words in "Dornan's ear might get them off their dead ass and get the rescue mission moving." Bo briefed the Congressman on the latest intelligence and explained his plan for *Grand Eagle*. Dornan promised to help in any way he could. He mentioned a meeting that was to be held the following week

Charles J. Patterson

Lieutenant Colonel James G. "Bo" Gritz

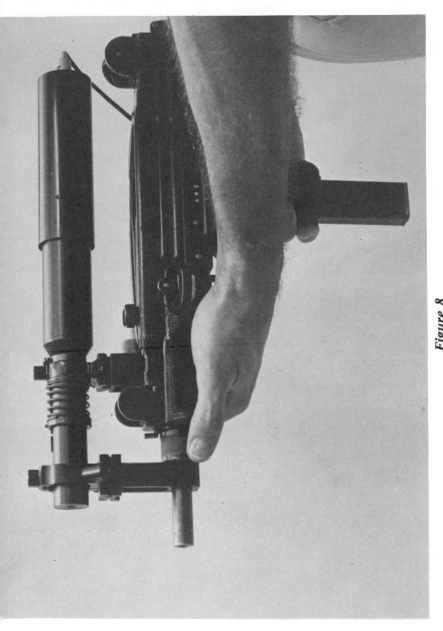

Figure 8
Laserscope Model FA-14A mounted on UZI Submachine gun

Chuck Patterson using Phoumano's office for prep.

Mekong River crossing site near That Phanom, Thailand.

where Admiral Paulson, Deputy Director of the DIA, and Admiral Bobby Inman, Deputy Director of Operations for the CIA, would be present. He said he would broach the subject with them and try to find out what the holdup was.

On December 8, the top-secret meeting was held in Washington between Congressman Dornan, Admiral Paulson and Admiral Inman. Dornan asked Inman what the holdup was on Bo Gritz's rescue mission. He said that he had met most of Gritz's men and they seemed fit and ready to go.

Inman was taken by surprise and expressed ignorance concerning *Operation Grand Eagle,* whereupon Paulson admitted that he had not deemed it necessary to inform the Deputy Director of the CIA.

Now, no man, particularly the Deputy Director of Operations for the CIA, likes to find out from a Congressman that his organization is involved in some covert activity which he not only knows nothing about—but that the Congressman is accusing him of stonewalling. The two admirals must have traded some strong words that day!

That night in Los Angeles, Gritz received a phone call from Cranston; Patterson listened on the extension. "The Admiral said you'll never get another God-damned penny out of us!" *Operation Grand Eagle* was dead; buried alongside of *Velvet Hammer!*

It is now time to consider the frustration that was boiling up in Bo Gritz. He was a hard-charging soldier, a man of action who had been "standing in the door" for almost three years waiting for the green light to go. All that time, he had been obsessed with one thought: "Rescue a POW!" Each day this obsession grew. It is easy to see why his mistrust of the "Washington crowd" was increasing. To him it must have seemed like they were deliberately trying to keep him from his calling (the rescue mission). To Bo, every day that he delayed could mean the life of one more prisoner (after all this time, the prisoners had to be deteriorating physically). He used to dream at night of the gaunt, starving figures holding out their hands to him—beckoning him to come and take them home! To a man like Bo Gritz, now thoroughly obsessed, nothing in this world was going to stop him—not even the government of the United States! The government turned him on to this project and, like a good soldier, he wasn't going to be turned off until he succeeded.

The final door was closed on *Operation Grand Eagle* when Gritz called Dunakoskie in Thailand and told him to bring the team home.

AUTHOR'S NOTE: Representative Robert Dornan, who headed the Congressional POW task force, said he believed the Gritz-Vang Pao plan had been backed by the government for a time. "When I asked for clarification of this at the highest intelligence, no one said it was untrue," Dornan said. "I was told, 'We're going another way now, Congressman.' It was indirect confirmation. They had decided that the Gritz plan was not feasible. Gritz is going public now because he believes the government has pulled the rug out from under him and I don't blame him."

The agency which Gritz calls the Activity does exist, but not by that name. It was established in the wake of the Iranian rescue mission's failure to prevent further disasters on future operations of this type. The organization was created to gather and act on its intelligence.

*Staff Sergeant Donald Sparks was captured
on 17 June 1969. He was originally classified as
"Missing in Action" but this was changed. A
letter from Sparks was found on the body of an
enemy soldier. It was dated April 1970, and
was addressed to his family in Iowa. One
would assume, after this letter became public,
that the Vietnamese would admit they had
Sparks. The Hanoi government claims they
know nothing about him.*

WILL BROWNELL
"Pawns of War", *Soldier of Fortune Magazine*,
Spring 1983

CHAPTER SIX

OPERATION LAZARUS

Patterson was almost overwhelmed with disappointment at the
negative turn of events. He figured that with the funding shutoff
from Washington, there was no way they could continue the mission. And to make matters worse, he did not even have a job to go
back to. He just couldn't understand how the "big-shot brass" in
Washington could play politics with men's lives. It seemed inconceivable that petty jealousies would take a back seat to the rescuing of American POWs.

Bo was only momentarily deterred. Driven by his personal obsession on the POW/MIA issue, he wasn't about to quit. He firmly
believed that if the POWs were ever to be rescued, he was the only
one that could do it—or would do it. The government had turned
him on to this thing and so far no one had officially turned him off.
Being the good soldier with a given mission, he was going to go!

"Don't worry," he said to his second-in-command, "We'll go
through the gawd-damned private sector and we'll get our money.
We'll get the money we need, no matter what we have to do. We'll
just have to delay our launch date a few months. Bo has spoken!"

There was a look in Gritz's eyes that said he meant every word
he was saying. Patterson knew from firsthand experience that Bo

was bull-headed, and anything he put his mind to, he accomplished. He decided that this was no time to desert his comrade. He would stick it out until the last shovel of dirt was thrown.

★   ★   ★

Gritz established a Chapter of the United Vietnam Veterans Organization (UVVO) which he called the "POW/MIA Never Forget Chapter." The primary purpose of the Chapter was to launder funds for the rescue mission and make contributions tax-free. All he had to do was submit the names of ten Vietnam Veterans as members along with $250 to the UVVO in Washington, D.C., and they sent him back the charter. This allowed him to collect donations legally and use the money to search for POW/MIAs. Once he had the charter, Bo and the other members of the team began to travel all over the U.S. begging for funds, promising "you give us the money and we'll get them out!"

The next thing on the agenda was equipment for the rescue mission: radios, weapons, packs, ammo, rations, uniforms, etc. Litton Industries, the nation's 11th largest defense contractor, donated $50,000 to the cause. As Gritz understood the transaction, the money was given to Litton by "certain people" in Washington who still maintained an "unofficial" interest in his mission. In turn, Gritz used the $50,000 to buy 14 ($1 million dollars' worth) of Litton's latest state-of-the-art "black boxes" or IDT boxes. These IDT (Indirect Transmission Devices—official military nomenclature: V/SIC MOSFETS) are book-sized secure transmitting and receiving devices with a built-in display screen. They can be attached to radios, teletypes, telecomputer firing systems and even the commercial telephone system. They provide a burst-coded transmission (a long message can be sent in a six-second burst). The operator can draw a map on the scale (screen) and it can be picked up on the other end. You can attach an IDT to a phone in one country and to a phone thousands of miles away and have secure transmissions.

The team was able to either beg, borrow, or scrounge other special equipment:
-- Four AN/PRC-74 radios. The Army's latest line of portable manpack radios which are compatible with the V/SIC MOSFETS.

-- One infrared scope. This device is attached to a weapon and when worn with the infrared goggles, puts a spot on the target during periods of darkness. Used as an aiming device. The infrared scope can burn out the retinas of a man's eye at 100 feet.

-- Night Vision Goggles. Battery powered goggles that can increase night vision by 100 percent. "It's like day at 100 yards!"

-- Three UZI submachine guns.

-- Two infrared (redeye) laser-scopes (Figure 8). These scopes cast a red dot on the target, allowing the dot to be seen at night with the naked eye. (During daylight hours the operator can get the same results with a special pair of goggles.) The size of the dot on the target depends on the distance from the target, i.e., quarter-sized at 100 yards. The weapon is zeroed so that the strike of the bullet coincides with the red dot at a given distance. Therefore, the weapon doesn't have to be aimed—just place the red dot on the target and fire. The device is extremely accurate. The laser-scopes procured by the Gritz team did not come from Litton Industries. As described by Patterson, they were probably the latest state of the art, Model FA-14A, from LASER DEFENSE SYSTEMS, Inc., of Little Rock, Arkansas. The FA-14A contains a helium neon laser that projects a small, red spot of intense light (laser) on an intended target. The system is small (14 inches long), light-weight (1.55 pounds including battery), and built to withstand rugged military combat conditions. It is powered by an AA flashlight battery and activated by a momentary pressure switch. At the time the *Lazarus* team received these lasers, the FA-14A was in limited use. Only a few highly classified agencies had it.— Other equipment collected included rucksacks, web gear (shoulder harness pistol belts, etc.), LRRP rations (Long Range Reconnaissance Patrol), compasses and camouflage (tiger suit) fatigues.

Fritz Mannes, a Marine veteran and actor Clint Eastwood's agent, was approached by Gritz and he promised to get the ex-Green Beret in touch with the popular screen star. Mannes said that he believed that once Clint heard the whole story he would surely want to help. That very night, Eastwood called Bo and invited them up to his Mount Shasta ranch. Several days later, a Warner Brother's jet flew Gritz and Patterson to the ranch.

Patterson was a great fan of Eastwood's and was, at first, somewhat awed by the actor's presence. Eastwood met them dressed in an old jogging outfit and Adidas tennis shoes—a stubble of beard showed on his face. He introduced them to actress Sondra Locke. Patterson thought she was even more beautiful in person than on the screen. Eastwood's pleasant manner soon put Patterson at ease.

Gritz briefed Eastwood on everything that had happened from the day General Aaron asked him to retire from the Army. He showed the actor some of the intelligence he had collected from his travels in SEA and several of the DIA documents his contacts had given him. Patterson then demonstrated some of the special equipment they were going to use, specifically the night vision goggles and the laser sights.

Eastwood was friendly and genuinely interested in what they had to say. After hearing Gritz's story and looking at the evidence, he offered to help in any way he could to rescue the American POWs.

Gritz asked the actor to do two things to help the rescue mission: First, he was to notify the President after Gritz and the team crossed the border into Laos; and second, get in touch with the President again after the rescue team had accessed a POW. According to Gritz's plan, Eastwood would meet with President Reagan the day after the team launched into Laos and inform the President that Gritz and his men were in the country seeking American POWs. Gritz believed that someone of Eastwood's stature could get directly through to the U.S. President and by-pass the "doorkeepers" who screened the President's visitors and information. Then, when they had freed an American POW or POWs, they would notify their base station in Thailand, which in turn would call the West Coast Communications Link in Los Angeles. L.A. would call Eastwood and the actor would tell the President that the team had rescued Americans. The President would be forced to take action to get them out "by sending rescue helicopters from the U.S. Seventh Fleet or by putting pressure on Thailand to effect a rescue."

Gritz had two alternate plans to exfiltrate Laos. The first was to push on across Laos and Vietnam (with any prisoners rescued) and rendezvous with a ship owned by Colonel Jack Bailey, a retired Air Force Colonel and fighter pilot. Gritz had met Bailey in Washington at a meeting of the National League of POW/MIA Families and talked the ex-Air Force officer into joining his rescue efforts. He sealed the deal by giving Bailey $5,000 for the use of his boat. Nicknamed "Acuna Jack" from the name of his refitted minesweeper, Bailey had been operating in the South China Sea for his own San Francisco-based charity called Operation Rescue. He used the ship to rescue Vietnamese "boat people" from pirates. Bailey also used the ship as a cover to gather information about any U.S. prisoners of war that the refugees claimed were still in captivity.

The other plan was basically to return to Thailand basically on the same route they used to go in. The healthy POWs would be brought along. Those not in good physical shape would be dropped off at friendly villages along the way. The villagers would care for them until they could be rescued.

AUTHOR'S NOTE: Why were Gritz and Patterson so reluctant to notify personnel in normal U.S. intelligence channels once they rescued an American POW? By this time, neither man trusted "our" own intelligence people. They believed the CIA or DIA would kill the freed prisoner(s), rather than have it known that they (the intelligence sector) knew about live POWs all these years and took no action. As Patterson put it, "The lying SOB's in our government have known all along that the POWs are there—yet they have done nothing! We couldn't take the chance of the wrong people getting their hands on any of our freed POWs."

Sean O'Toolis, an IRA gunrunner who has spent considerable time in Vietnam purchasing arms for the Irish Republican Army, claims that he talked to a group of American POWs in Laos who said they were afraid to return home because they feel they have been betrayed in their own country and would be killed before they could compromise the DIA's position.[1]

---

[1] Alex McColl and Bill Guthrie, "Blarney"; (The Southeast Asian Saga of an IRA Gunrunner), *Soldier of Fortune*, Spring 1981.

Eastwood agreed to help them and, surprisingly, agreed to write a check for $30,000. He mailed it to Bo a few days later and asked for nothing in return. His only request was that his name be kept out of it. There is no doubt that the actor was motivated solely by a strong sense of patriotism and a desire to help free his imprisoned countrymen.

A week later, Sergeant Dick Clark, a friend of Bo's with the L.A. Police Department, introduced them to William Shatner on the set of "T. J. Hooker." Over lunch, they explained the proposed mission. Shatner was enthusiastic about the project. He promptly agreed to help, but he wanted his attorneys to write an agreement for him to have the book and movie rights. A few days later, Gritz received a check for $10,000 through the mail, along with a letter of agreement giving Shatner the book and movie rights. Bo promptly banked the check and laughed as he tore up the letter of agreement.

AUTHOR'S NOTE: In an interview published in the *LA Times* on January 2, 1983, Shatner was quoted as saying:
"I was introduced to Mr. Gritz several months ago and became intrigued by his story because I had an ongoing story-development deal at Paramount—to buy stories that I found interesting. What he was going to do with the money was none of my business," he said, but added that Gritz told him he was "contemplating a POW rescue mission."
"The man is a fascinating man!" Shatner said.

In mid-January, Patterson walked into Gritz's office and found him reading a copy of *The New York Daily World*, the newspaper of the American Communist Party. "Reading the comics?" Patterson asked.

"That dirty son-of-a-bitch!" exclaimed Gritz. He handed the paper to Patterson. "Look what Scott Barnes did!"

The paper featured an article about Barnes' exploits in Thailand and about *Operation Bohica!*

"I knew it!" said Patterson. "I had a feeling about that guy. Well, he's dead meat now!"

When Scott Barnes returned to the U.S., he contacted several TV and newspaper personalities including Ted Koppel of ABC-TV's "Nightline" and the *Washington Post*'s Jack Anderson. They both interviewed him and decided that he was a "lying weirdo." His tales were so incredible that only four publications printed his story: *The New York Daily World*, the newspaper of the American Communist Party; the Hermosa Beach, *EASY Rider*, a motorcycle magazine; a Canadian paper, the *Vancouver Herald*; and the *Covert Action Information Bulletin*, a leftist publication which concentrates on exposing United States intelligence operations.

In the articles, Barnes claimed that he was contacted by one of Gritz's men in April 1981, and told to get ready for a "top secret invasion of Laos" to free American POWs. He says the reason he was contacted was because he was a close friend of both General Vang Pao and Congressman Robert Dornan; and that it was he, in fact, who "arranged for the first meeting between Gritz and Vang Pao, in the Congressman's office."

Barnes says that he and another man from *Operation Grand Eagle* crossed over the border into Laos near Mahaxay and confirmed that there were two Americans being held there. He claims that they received a message from the CIA that directed them to kill the two Americans. These were the same two CIA agents he says were captured in Laos planting "yellow rain," so the U.S. could blame it on the Communists. Allegedly, he and the other man were issued AR-180 rifles with silencers to make the kill—but he refused to kill fellow Americans. Instead, he returned to the United States because he believed the CIA was going to kill him.

Patterson and Gritz were angered by the publications, but Barnes' story was so preposterous they knew no one would believe it. That fact probably saved him from reprisal; however, he still had to look over his shoulder. Barnes dropped out of sight and neither Gritz nor Patterson saw him again.

★   ★   ★

By this time, several more people had joined the venture and were actively engaged in fund raising:

-- Gary Goldman: Ex-Army Captain who served in the Infantry in Vietnam. Goldman was a marathoner and kept in top physical condition.

-- Lance Trimmer: An ex-Special Forces Communications Specialist, now working in civilian life as a private detective in Montana.

-- William Batchelor: Ex-Army Security Agent and retired Master Sergeant. Batchelor helped in fund raising and ran the Communications Link East, from his home in Washington, D.C.

-- Lynn Standerwick: POW daughter who worked in fundraising and helped run the East Communication Link. There was every indication that Lynn's father was dead. According to the afteraction report, her father's copilot was positive that her father was shot right after the crash. A North Vietnamese guard was carrying his watch and dog-tags. Still, this young lady gave freely of her time to help the mission.

-- Janet Townley: Another POW daughter who worked hard in fundraising and helped run the East Coast Communication Link. Janet's case was different because the family had pictures after his capture of her father lying on a hospital bed with a broken arm. He was not repatriated in 1973; there was a possibility that her father might still be alive.

★ ★ ★

Lance Trimmer took Lynn Standerwick and Janet Townley back to Montana with him where they helped him work on insurance fraud cases. They offered to donate any commissions they made to the rescue mission. Altogether, they raised over $10,000! There was one particular case worthy of mentioning.

Farmer Brown lived on a small farm and was drawing total disability. "He couldn't even raise his hand off the table!" The insurance company suspected he was faking but they were never able to prove it. Farmer Brown was a wily fellow. Lance Trimmer took the case as a challenge. Janet and Lynn, dressed in their tightest jeans and sexiest low-cut blouses, drove their car to Farmer Brown's and stopped short of his driveway. Lynn got out and let the air out of one of the tires. Then they drove the car into

Farmer Brown's and parked. There they were—two defenseless ladies with a flat and willing to do anything to get some help. Both walked up on the porch and Lynn knocked at the door. It took poor incapacitated Farmer Brown several minutes to hobble to the door. He parted the curtains and looked out and his eyes feasted. When the door opened, he was standing there, straight and strong, looking very macho.

Janet gave him her best we-need-your-help look. "We're sorry to bother you, but we're desperate. We have a flat tire and no jack. Can you please help us? We would be ever so grateful."

Farmer Brown let his eyes slide down the well-defined curves and back up to the ample cleavage showing. He almost drooled on his shirt.

He nodded, "I'd be glad to help you."

The girls tried to let their eyes and bodies speak a silent language of possible rewards.

Farmer Brown almost double-timed to get a jack from his garage. He tore into the task of changing the tire like a man possessed, as, unknown to him, secreted cameras clicked away.

He received his reward, and needless to say, the gallant hero is no longer drawing disability!

The team established two stateside communication links, using teletype, the public telephone system and the IDT secure transmission devices. Lynn and Janet were to run the Communications Link East in the home of William Batchelor, in Washington, D.C. They were to be known as "Angels East." The West Coast Link was set up in Gritz's home in L.A. and was run by Claudia and retired Sergeant Major Ramon Rodriguiz. They were "Angels West." Once they were in Thailand, this setup would allow them to have secure communications from their launch site with the West Coast and Clint Eastwood, as well as Washington.

By the 10th of August 1982, almost three years after retiring, almost three long years of frustrations, postponements, and tribulations, Gritz finally believed he had the organization that could do the job, and the equipment and money to go ahead with the rescue mission. This time he did not have even the quasi-backing of the U.S. Government. But now he felt that this was a possible advantage—not to have the bureaucratic restraints of government. Besides, he was positive that the government would embrace him with loving arms when he returned with a POW.

The final organization of *Operation Lazarus* was as follows:

Bo Gritz . . . . Commander
Chuck Patterson . . . . Executive Officer
Jim Donahue . . . . Medic
Gary Goldman . . . . Commo

Support Team
Thailand:
Gordon Wilson . . . . Liaison
Jack Bailey . . . . Liaison
Lance Trimmer . . . . Commo
Scott Weekly . . . . Commo
Butch Jones . . . . Commo/Liaison
United States:
Vinnie Arnone . . . . Liaison/Fundraising
Larry Palma . . . . Fundraising
Angels East . . . . Batchelor, Townley, Standerwick
Angels West . . . . Claudia Gritz, Rodriguiz

★　　　　　★　　　　　★

"Acuna Jack" Bailey, the retired Air Force Colonel involved with the rescue of boat people, was supposed to introduce Gritz and Patterson to his good friend General Phoumi Nosavon, former Deputy Premier of Laos, now living in exile in Bangkok. In addition, he was going to "grease the skids" with his friends in Thai customs so the weapons and equipment could be smuggled into the country.

When Washington closed the door on him, Gritz decided to discontinue his association with General Vang Pao. He had come to respect the General and trusted his intelligence; however, he believed that Vang Pao was a CIA man first and therefore he couldn't be trusted. Gritz had met Phoumi Nosavon several months earlier, and Jack Bailey had several ongoing operations with the old warlord. Most important to Gritz was the fact that Phoumi Nosavon was on the outs with the CIA, so he could be trusted not to give away their plans.

Sean O'Toolis, an IRA Gunrunner, claims that in 1981, he visited five prison camps with Americans in them. Bon Song was the biggest with at least 40 Americans; another 12 were imprisoned at Samtue, Laos; another 12 were bound in a bamboo cage, inside a cave near Sopsan, Laos; another 38 at a camp near Lakso (he didn't know whether it was in Laos or Vietnam)—the major difference in the 1981 tour was that over half the prisoners had apparently died since his visit in 1979. "They looked like death warmed over. Their weight averaged about 100 pounds, and many seemed sick."

ALEX MCCOLL and BILL GUTHRIE
"Blarney" (The Saga of a SEA IRA Gunrunner),
SOF, Spring 1981.

CHAPTER SEVEN

Gritz named his latest venture *Operation Lazarus*—after the biblical character raised from the dead by Jesus. Based on intelligence gathered during *Operation Grand Eagle*, a tentative target was selected on Phu Xun mountain, just Southwest of Sepone, Laos. Sepone (also spelled Tchepone) is located on a major road junction in eastern Laos, more than 160 miles from Nakhon Phanom, Thailand. According to reports brought back by Vang Pao's people, there were 120 Americans being held in this small prison camp. The prisoners were kept in a cave complex at night and brought out to tend crops during the day. However, before a final decision was made on the target, Gritz believed that the area needed to be reconnoitered again. He was hoping to use Phoumi Nosavon's men for this mission.

The advance party, consisting of Gritz, Patterson, and Jack Bailey, arrived in Bangkok on 14 September 1982, at 2300 hours. The main body was due to commence infiltrating Thailand one week later. They were to be disguised as tourists to avoid detection and would be smuggling in the arms and equipment.

The three members of the advance party took a taxi to the Federal Hotel. The Federal was not very fancy but it was comfortable, reasonable, inconspicuous, and filled with Americans, Englishmen, and Australians taking leave from jobs in the Middle East. The hotel caters to "farangs" (foreigners), and every delight known and imagined by man is available for the right price. A patron may bring his own woman, or the hotel will furnish one for about 500 bhat (for all night—around 19 American dollars). They even have a special deal where you can get two gals for 750 bhat, but a man has to be pretty virile for that. Shortly after their arrival, Bailey took off to spend the night with his girl friend, a hooker who worked at the Three Sister's Bar.

The next morning, Phoumano Nosavon, the old General's son, picked them up in a taxi and they drove out to Phoumi's home. Phoumano was a former Colonel in the Laotian Air Force and took his pilot training in America. He works for a French news service and owns a firm that provides Thai laborers to the Middle East.

Phoumi's home is a large two-story bungalow in the suburbs of Bangkok. The house is surrounded by an eight-foot wall, the top of which is embedded with jagged broken glass (a common practice in the Orient to discourage intruders). The guard at the gate, armed with an M-16 rifle, saluted as they sped through.

General Phoumi Nosavon was Deputy Premier of Laos in the mid-1960s. He was supported by the U.S. Central Intelligence Agency until they caught him skimming off the top of monies they gave him for arms and supplies to fight the Communists. Now he runs a weak, shadowy Laotian government in exile and nurses dreams of grandeur about "retaking" Laos from the Communists. His people control several strongholds in his homeland and are still actively fighting the Pathet Lao (Laotian "Reds" or Communists) and Vietnamese.

The general met them in his "War Room," its walls filled with maps showing the disposition of his forces in Laos. At first glance one would think that he already had complete control of his homeland. Although Phoumi speaks and understands English, he chose to speak only in Thai. (Thai is also the dominant language in Laos.) This is a common practice by so-called dignitaries in the Orient.

They seem to believe that it is loss of face to speak another language. If you want to talk with them, you either speak their language or go through the formalities of an interpreter. In this case, Patterson, who speaks fluent Thai, acted as interpreter for Gritz.

Phoumi was short and fat and appeared to be in his late sixties or early seventies. His son Phoumano was a chip off the old block—he was fat, too.

The ex-Deputy Premier had been thoroughly briefed about the American's proposed mission, so after a short period of formalities —drinking tea and making polite small talk—Gritz got down to business: "General, my group of Special Forces wants to locate American Prisoners of War which we believe are being held by the Communists, and we would like your help."

"Yes, I get many such reports of Americans in Laos," returned the warlord, "and I will, of course, give whatever help I can. I have many soldiers in my homeland that I can order to help you; but you must understand, I am very limited in equipment and supplies. Will your country help provide resources to my Liberation Fighters?"

"Yes, General, we can help some, but our assets are limited."

"Your government is behind you on this operation, isn't it?" asked Phoumi.

"Yes, Sir—but not openly. Because of the political situation, the U.S. Government cannot come out into the open on this operation."

The two leaders negotiated for some time and finally several agreements were reached: Phoumi agreed to furnish an armed escort to the target area and 500 soldiers for the rescue mission. He promised to send out runners immediately to his ground commanders and have them report to Bangkok to prepare for the mission. In return he asked for uniforms, weapons, medical supplies and food for his people in the refugee camps. He asked for an initial sum of $7,000. Gritz assured him that he would get the money. The General asked if the Americans could help him set up a radio communication network so he could talk to his commanders in Laos. (Phoumi depended on the ancient, but reliable method of runners to get messages back and forth.) Gritz said that he had the capability to grant this. The shrewd old warlord asked Gritz to leave him all the American equipment after the operation was over. The former Green Beret Colonel agreed to leave everything but the "supersecret black communication boxes;" these he said he "had to turn back over to the CIA."

Finally, Phoumi delivered his high impact demand. "I am trying to get a loan from Arab-American banks so that I can mount an offensive and liberate my country from the Communists, and Mr. Bailey said that you would get your government to help."

Gritz and Patterson were surprised; this was the first they had heard of any loan. Gritz thought fast, "I would be glad to help, and I know my government will help you if we are successful on this mission. How much money are we talking about?"

"One billion dollars," returned Phoumi, "to be repaid back with interest and concessions when we liberate Laos."

Gritz and Patterson almost fell off their chairs. The old man was living in a dream world. No one, not even Arabs, are going to fork over $1 billion to an old has-been who has only promises and dreams for collateral. Gritz danced on. "When I return to America I will contact my superiors in Washington and ask them to help. I also know some influential people in the banking business in Los Angeles. You must be patient—this is a great deal of money."

When Gritz and Patterson left Phoumi Nosavon, they felt good about the meeting. The old general seemed to know what he was talking about and he seemed sincere. At long last, and without government assistance, it looked like a "GO" for *Operation Lazarus*.

"I wish to hell Bailey would quit promising things he can't deliver," Gritz said to his second-in-command. "Now we're going to have to be careful and not piss off Phoumi. I guess we'll have to string him along about the bank loan. No one is going to give him $1 billion. We'll have to try to keep him satisfied until the operation is over. I think I can come up with some false papers in the States. Who knows? If we're successful, maybe Uncle Sam will give him some money—as a reward."

Gritz and Bailey were scheduled to return to the USA the next day to start the main body on its way. Patterson was to remain behind and look for a good safehouse in Bangkok, and set up liaison with Phoumi.

When Gritz bounced Bailey about the "loan surprise," Bailey said he had to promise the general their assistance in order to get any cooperation. Gritz, Bailey and Patterson all decided they felt "comfortable" with Phoumi Nosavon.

That evening, the three of them decided to go out on the town for dinner and a few drinks. The first place they visited was the Three Sister's Bar in Patpong (a district/suburb of Bangkok), where "Papason" Bailey was welcomed with open arms. There are two major districts in the city that cater to farangs—Patpong and Soi Cowboy. During the Vietnam War, thousands of American GI's took their R&R (Rest and Recuperation Leave) in Bangkok. Business has dropped off some since the Americans departed SEA—but there is still a heavy influx of foreigners from the Middle East. Flesh is still peddled by the pound and some of it is damn good looking: beautiful, tiny, kewpie dolls with dark eyes and long black hair, set off by smooth "cafe-au-lait bodies" skilled in the art of making a man enjoy the pleasures of the Orient.

Each bar has anywhere from 10 to 20 hostesses and most have live entertainment. The hostesses sit with guests, drink their tea, and get a percentage of each drink the guests buy. If a customer falls under the charm of one of the young ladies and becomes temporarily in love, he can persuade the young lady to spend the night with him for a price. He pays the bar owner a stipend of 100 bhat ($4.00) and the lady for her services (500 bhat, going price). Of course, a gentleman usually buys a lady breakfast.

They caught a taxi in Patpong and went to Soi Cowboy. The first bar one sees there, after exiting the taxi, is the Chitra II Cocktail Lounge or Suzie's. Suzie's is known throughout SEA as having a fine stable of delicious women. They by-passed Suzie's and went straight to the Heavenly Bar, an old Special Forces hangout. They barged in expecting to see a familiar face or at least a familiar "ass." They found it was still a soldier's hangout, but the new patrons spoke Spanish. They walked into a room filled with about 100 Cubans, who were themselves on R&R from Vietnam and Laos. It's strange, but some things never change. The bar was still a soldier's hangout and the soldiers were serving in the same countries, but now they wore a different uniform and spoke a different language—and they were on the opposite side of the ideological fence. The Americans had one quick drink and headed to Suzie's.

Early the next morning, Patterson was awakened by a loud

rapping at his door. He awoke slowly to a fuzzy, cobweb world; his mouth was dry. "Yeah. Who's there?"

"It's me, Bo. Open up and let me in."

Patterson looked at his watch. It was only 7:00 a.m. "Shit!" he mumbled, and rolled off the bed. He staggered sleepily to the door, unlocked the latch and swung it open. "It's too damn early! What's up?"

An enraged Gritz was standing there shaking his head. The retired lieutenant colonel pushed past Patterson and strode into the room.

"What's the matter?" asked the puzzled Patterson, closing the door and turning toward his leader.

"You'll never believe what that ignorant son-of-a-bitch Bailey did!"

"What now?"

"He gets on the damned phone to the States and tells the whole fucking world, in the clear, 'Hey it's a go. We're going to get the POWs and bring them home!'—right over the gawd-damned telephone, where God and the whole world can hear!"

Patterson immediately came uncorked, and when Bailey walked in a few seconds later, he jumped up and confronted the retired officer. "Jack, if this operation gets fucked up because of you and your big mouth—the whole world is not big enough for you to hide. I will come kill you!"

The red-faced Bailey yelled back, "Are you threatening me?"

"Me? Fuck no! I'm promising you—I will come kill you! You know better than to get on the line to the States and talk in the clear. What the hell is the matter with you? Do you want to blow everything?"

"I wasn't thinking straight; I was just happy that we are finally going," Bailey answered, his voice toning down.

"Well you better start thinking, 'cause it's my ass that's on the line—not yours. You're gonna be sitting on your safe ass in Washington doing fundraising, while our asses will be hanging in the wind."

There was a real danger now that they were compromised; however, Gritz decided to go on with things as planned.

The clash between Patterson and Bailey was inevitable. Patterson didn't trust the ex-colonel and he couldn't stand phonies. "Jack

Bailey was a phoney. He drank too much. He was a loudmouth and a braggart. He was always promising things he couldn't deliver."

A few hours later, Phoumano picked up Gritz and Bailey to take them to the airport. Bailey hadn't said a word since the argument. Patterson realized that he would never be able to trust the ex-colonel again.

It was apparent that the old General's son was also depressed. Gritz asked Phoumano, "What's the matter with you—you don't look happy today."

"I am very sad," answered Phoumano. "I have people fighting in Laos who are hungry and have no medical supplies. I need money to bring the commanders down to Bangkok, so I can brief them on the American rescue mission."

"I thought that your father had already sent for them," said Gritz.

"Oh yes. They are on their way—but additional expenses have come up."

"Are you handling part of the operation for your father?"

"Yes. He is too old to go to the field. So I do all the field operation work for him."

Gritz turned to Patterson. "Better give him a couple of thousand."

Patterson reached into his pocket, pulled out the roll of expense money and counted out $2,000 in American greenbacks.

Phoumano snatched it out of the ex-sergeant's hand and counted it quickly. He was suddenly in a much more amiable mood.

Figure 9
Map given to Patterson by Phoumi Nosavon,
former Deputy Premier of Laos.

*During the French-IndoChina War 1946 to
1954, some 37,000 French Colonial soldiers
were captured by the Communists in Vietnam,
Laos and Cambodia. Less than 3,700 were
repatriated, leaving some 33,000 unaccounted
for. Throughout the last 28 years the French
have been blackmailed into paying up to
$50,000 per set of remains, for a total thus far
exceeding $700 million in ransom and grave
maintenance.*

CHAPTER EIGHT

Patterson spent the next few days househunting with Phoumano
Nosavon. They needed a house large enough to accommodate
eight to ten people. He finally found a bungalow that would serve
their purpose on Soi Sepon (Sepon Street). It was owned by one of
Bangkok's police chiefs. The chief asked the American why he
needed such a large house. Patterson told him that he had several
friends coming, all Vietnam veterans, and they were going to have
a reunion. This seemed to satisfy the chief. Patterson payed $1,200
for three months' rent.

On 23 December, Phoumi Nosavon handed Patterson a map of
Laos on which was indicated the location of a 1966 U.S. air crash
and two American POW camps (page 66). One of the camps was
located near Tchepone (Sepone) on Phu Xun mountain. According
to Phoumi's sources, 120 Americans were being held there. This
information coincided with intelligence given them earlier by
General Vang Pao.

During the next few days, Patterson kept as low a profile as
possible. Believing that Phoumano was representing his father, he
worked with the ex-pilot each day. Among other things,
Phoumano was involved in the business of contracting Thai laborers for the Middle East, particularly Saudi Arabia. This is legal but
one of the most crooked scams in the Orient. Thailand has major
economic problems so jobs are difficult to come by. There is still
competition for the high-paying overseas jobs. Phoumano pays
money to Middle East companies to allow him to select their

workers, then turns around and collects the first three months' salary from the workers he hires. It's tantamount to slave labor.

As the days went by, Patterson noticed some changes taking place in Phoumano's office. New desks, new rugs, and a new photocopy machine appeared. Phoumano's business must be good. At the same time, not one of Phoumi's guerrilla chiefs showed up from Laos.

"They come soon, Sergeant Patterson," promised Phoumano, "they come soon. Maybe tomorrow!"

It finally began to dawn on Patterson that he was getting the inscrutable Oriental run-around. Feeling increasingly discouraged about the Phoumi Nosavon and son situation, he picked up the phone and called Loh Tharaphant in Nakhon Phanom.

Loh, an acquaintance of Bo's, was an ethnic Vietnamese born in Hanoi, and now was a Thai citizen. He ran an underground railroad smuggling people in and out of Laos and had numerous contacts throughout Laos with the Free Lao who were fighting the Communists.

Bo had recruited Loh as an agent the year before, when he was in Thailand running down POW leads.

Loh answered the phone and Patterson identified himself.

"I'm glad you called!" announced Loh. "I would like to meet with you. I have some very important information for Mr. Bo."

"If you come to Bangkok, I would be glad to pay your way," offered Patterson. "If you can't make it down here, I'll try to get up to Nakon Phanom."

"That's not necessary," returned Loh. "I have a son in Bangkok and I can meet you at his home on Saturday. He lives at 2495 Soi Kanom."

Patterson generally did not like the Vietnamese but he warmed to Loh immediately. His instinct was usually right, and it told him he could trust Loh Tharaphant.

"I have many connections with the Free Lao guerrillas," offered Loh. "I know they will work with you if you give them medical supplies and food. Many of their families are in refugee camps in Thailand. They go into Laos to conduct intelligence missions for the Thai Government, and sometimes they go just to kill Communists. The Communists drove them out of their lands and forced many of them into slave labor. They like Americans; most of them fought on the U.S. side during the war."

The Free Lao forces that Loh was talking about have no connection with Phoumi Nosavon's people or Vang Pao's. They are from smaller independent tribes of mountain people. The Laotian Governments have never been able to overcome tribal loyalty and tie the nation together. The various tribes have been fighting each other for generations. The Montagnards, or mountain people, have never recognized a border between Laos and Vietnam. Stronger chiefs dominate weaker ones. In effect, the country is run by a group of warlords and lesser subordinate chiefs. Power is established strictly by force of arms.

Loh assured Patterson that he could get several of the separate Free Lao guerrilla chiefs to cooperate and assist the American rescue attempt. "General Phoumi Nosavon and his son are very big crooks and should not be trusted! They will steal your money!" he warned.

Before he left, Bo told Patterson that he believed Loh could be trusted, though apparently the Vietnamese flunked a lie detector test given to him about a year ago by DIA operative, Jim Hurt. However, Bo said there were extenuating circumstances. "Loh will be our ace in the hole if our deal with Phoumi falls through," he told Patterson. "So contact Loh while I'm gone and evaluate his potential."

Patterson was rapidly becoming disillusioned with Phoumi and son and was beginning to look upon Loh as the best choice. He had a gut feeling that Loh was right about the Nosavons.

★   ★   ★

The remainder of the team began filtering in, one and two at a time. Because all of the equipment was now being smuggled in, this was a tense period. Patterson met each member of the team and watched them sweat it out as they brought the equipment through Thai customs. The Thai customs people are inconsistent, especially when it comes to Americans. Sometimes they just smile and wave you through; other times they will check every inch of your luggage. Appearance of the traveler has a great deal to do with their attitude. A person who looks like a hippy is usually searched very thoroughly.

One incident of note occurred in the U.S. before the team deployed. Lance Trimmer and Gary Goldman were checking out the radios and IDT boxes, between Clint Eastwood's Shasta ranch and Redding, California. A deputy sheriff became suspicious when he noted Trimmer sitting in his car by the side of the road with a long antenna sticking out of the back window. The ex-Special Forces Communicator was arrested and taken to Redding. There were a few "hairy" hours until "Dirty Harry" was able to make a few phone calls and squelch the incident.

The last two members coming into Thailand were bringing the radios and IDT boxes.

"No problem! No problem!" exclaimed Bailey, "I know the chief customs agent. He'll walk the radios right through. No problem."

The first major glitch in the operation came when Bailey's contact in Thai customs proved unable or unwilling to look the other way when the two men tried to walk through with the sophisticated communications equipment. The "no problem" became a big problem! The radios were discovered and confiscated and the two men were arrested.

Gritz was furious! He was beginning to think that Bailey was nothing but hot air.

Patterson's growing dislike for Acuna Jack grew some more. "NO PROBLEM? My ass! Jack, how did you ever make Colonel?"

Finally, the Thai customs agent agreed to release the men and radios, provided the Americans would take the communications equipment back out of the country. Apparently the Thais really didn't want to make a big stink. They didn't know what the crazy Americans were up to and they wanted no part of it. They just wanted the radios to disappear. And they no doubt hoped the Americans would disappear, too.

The resourceful Bo Gritz came through again. Apparently through his ex-wife, he had some Chinese Mafia contacts in Kuala Lampur, Malaysia. He teletyped a message to Yap Ching Quee, a

Tong leader. Yap Ching agreed to handle the equipment. Gary Goldman flew with the equipment to Kuala Lampur where Yap Ching met him and smuggled the material through Malaysia customs. Then he reboxed the radios and IDT boxes and sent them back to Thailand where Gritz was forced to pay a "black tax" (bribe) of $700 to get them back.

Finally, with everyone on board and equipment in hand, the *Lazarus* team members settled into their assigned tasks. A few days after he arrived, Jim Donahue, who was to be the Ground Team Medic, had to return to the States because his wife became ill. Gritz was furious! He was so obsessed with the task at hand that he believed Donahue should have put the mission ahead of his wife. This was a "traitorous act" as far as he was concerned. Donahue was replaced by Dominic Zappone. Dominic was not a combat veteran but he served in the Special Forces with Gritz in Panama. At first, Patterson was worried about Bo's choice, because "Zap" was not a combat veteran.

"He's a body; he's been trained and we need another man. We might as well pop his cherry!" declared Gritz.

The other members of the team in country were Lance Trimmer, Gary Goldman, Scott Weekly, Jack Bailey and Gordon Wilson. Weekly, whose nickname was "Doctor Death", was a former Navy SEAL and a genius when it came to electronics and weapons. In the States, "Angels East" and "Angels West" were standing by.

It didn't take the Americans long to find out the true colors of General Phoumi Nosavon and his son Phoumano. Color them thieves! This is something the CIA had found out ten years earlier. Patterson briefed Gritz on the happenings in his absence. Bo was disappointed that nothing had been accomplished on the Nosavon end. Phoumano gave him the same run-around that he had been giving Patterson: "Men come soon from Lao, maybe tomorrow."

Bo went through the motions of negotiating the loan for Phoumi while he was in the U.S. One bank he approached through a friend in L.A. turned him down cold, but he didn't want the old warlord to find that out. It was necessary to string along Phoumi for a while. He asked for a meeting with Phoumi to discuss the loan. Once inside the ex-Premier's exalted presence, he asked, "Hey, where are these people from Laos we are supposed to meet with? We are tired of hearing 'soon' or 'maybe tomorrow'. My people are all here and we are ready to go. We have given you the $7,000 we agreed upon—but we don't see any results!"

Phoumi Nosavon shrugged his inscrutable shoulders. "You have not given me $7,000. You gave my son $7,000. I have received only $1,000. You must not trust my son. He is a thief!"

It suddenly dawned on Patterson! The new office furniture and equipment in Phoumano's office! It was purchased with the money that was supposed to go to Phoumi! He should have caught on sooner. Loh was right. He had warned him. That little fat bastard had stolen their money!

Gritz burst out, "We thought your son was your representative! We've been working here getting ready for this operation for almost two months. This is a hell-of-a-time to find out that your son is a crook. Why didn't you warn us?"

Phoumi showed no emotion. "I thought you knew. Anyway, I will need more money if I am to bring my commanders down from Laos."

Gritz didn't know what to say. He couldn't do what he felt like doing, nor could he say what he wanted to say. Even a blind man could see they had been snookered. He held his breath for an instant and tried to calm down. They were too far into the mission for him to blow it with a temper tantrum. Anyway, it probably wouldn't do any good. He asked, "How soon can you get your commanders here?"

"Soon, maybe next week. I am very sorry about the money. I will talk to my son. But I am very pleased that you are getting the loan for me."

ພຣະຣາຊອານາຈັກລາວ

KINGDOM OF LAOS
THE UNITED LAO PEOPLE FRONT
FOR THE LIBERATION OF LAOS
(UFLLL)

Mr. Leni C. Palmani
International Financier
International Society of Financiers
Chairman, Interfunds Asia
Hongkong

Dear Mr. Palmani

We confirm our meeting today in Siam Inter Continental Hotel that the
Kingdom of Laos is prepared to accept funds from your lending group
the amount of USD1,000 Millions based on terms and conditions furnished
to MR. VICTOR LAVALEE in Los Angeles California.

We also confirm that MR. LAVALEE has the complete documents in his hand
to negotiate with full authority.

Thank you.

Very truly yours,

GENERAL PHOUMI NOSAVAN
Prime Minister President of
Council Kingdom of Laos

Done in Bangkok Thailand

WITNESSES:

Figure 10
Phoumi Nosavon's one billion dollar loan letter.

*At Sepone in Laos, there is a prison camp
where there are 100 Americans and two
Frenchmen. The Frenchmen are not guarded
because their minds are gone. They just wander
around. The POWs are locked in bamboo cages
at night inside a cave complex. I asked one
American to come with me and I would help
him escape—but he just broke down and cried!*

AKHEIN, Montagnard guerrilla chief whose
village is located near Sepone

CHAPTER NINE

Gritz, Patterson, Wilson and Weekly held a meeting that night at
the team bungalow. "I have decided to break with Phoumi
Nosavon and go with Loh Tharaphant's people," announced Gritz,
decisively.

"Good decision, Bo," chipped in Patterson. "I think we can trust
Loh. He impresses the hell out of me. I just don't trust that fat
fucker Phoumano or his father. It is hard for me to believe that
that old man was once the Prime Minister of Laos. What about
Bailey, he's Phoumi's boy."

"What about him?" returned Gritz. "I'll just send him back to
the States to work on fund raising—then we'll cut him out of the
net."

"What are we going to do to Phoumano?" asked Scott Weekly.

"Nothing now," Gritz answered. "I'd like to. I'd like to take him
out. But we can't now. We have to string him along with Phoumi
for the time being. We have to find accommodations up north, and
we have to get our equipment out of Phoumi's place. I talked to
Loh on the phone today. He's coming down tomorrow so we can
start making plans. I don't want Phoumi to know we have cut him
out until we are already in country."

Lance Trimmer and Gordon Wilson left the next morning to go
north and search for a communications base and safehouse. An
invitation arrived for the Americans to attend the grand opening

of Phoumano Nosavon's new office, scheduled for the 25th of October. A Buddhist monk was to bless the office, after which there were to be refreshments. Patterson figured that this occasion might be a good time for a little payback to Phoumano for stealing their money. During the war he taught survival at the Green Beret School at Payaa, Thailand. This required a special skill in snake handling which he learned in a course at the cobra farm, just outside Bangkok. He could attest to the danger of a cobra, having been bitten once while teaching a class. It was a morning when he had a classic hangover. He was showing the class how you could paralyze a cobra by pinching the snake at the 10th vertebra. This causes the snake to keep its hood spread and face forward. His hangover caused his hand to be sweaty and as he was picking up the deadly serpent, his hand slipped! The cobra struck him in the jaw. The pain shot across his face as the fangs bit deep. Then the snake crawled onto his back with its tail wrapped around his legs. He froze, waiting for the next strike. His eyes zeroed in on his assistant instructor and he spoke very slowly so as not to cause the snake to strike: "Get the snake off my back!"

The assistant instructor shook his head, "Fuck you! I'm not grabbing no snake!"

"Get a stick and knock this snake off my back!"

One of the students picked up a stick and flicked off the snake.

Patterson saved his own life because he had been taught to handle the bite of a cobra. He injected himself with 5cc of cobra serum intravenously (which was always on hand) and another 5cc around the bite. He lived, but he was sick for a week. The first three days were the worst. Every nerve ending in his body throbbed with pain. There was nothing he could do. He had to just gut it out. Patterson could visualize Phoumano going through the same thing! That would be a coup!

The day before the Grand Opening celebration, Patterson went to the local market and purchased a five-foot Asian cobra and stuck it in a small suitcase. Early the next morning he let himself into Phoumano's office and placed the deadly snake in the fat Laotian's middle desk drawer. He figured that when Phoumano opened the drawer, the snake would either strike him, or at the very least, the Laotian would piss all over himself.

Later that morning, several of the Americans were sitting downstairs in Phoumano's reception room drinking coffee and acting very innocent. Phoumano arrived about 9:00 a.m. with his hench-men and the Bhuddist monk. The entourage went directly up-stairs to the Laotian's office. Apparently they were going to do a little business before the ceremony. Patterson looked at Goldman and winked. Meanwhile, upstairs, the snake had somehow crawled out of the desk drawer and was now positioned beneath Phouma-no's new black leather couch, upon which two henchmen and the Bhuddist monk sat. The monk felt something slide between his bare legs and looked down to see the five-foot cobra slithering out from under the couch. Someone yelled "SNAKE," and the result was the same as if someone in a San Diego shirt factory had yelled "IMMIGRATION!" Amidst screams of terror, the office was va-cated faster than a speeding bullet, as five overweight business-men and one skinny monk tried to come down the three-foot-wide stairs at the same time. The result was a tumbling mass of terror-ized humanity. The Bhuddist monk was tangled in his robes and everyone else was tangled with the monk. It took a few minutes for the pandemonium to subside to a roar. The monk was fright-ened because a snake is considered a bad omen. He refused to bless the office and left in a huff, mumbling to himself. Phoumano was shaking like strawberry jello. The Americans could hardly restrain their laughter. Patterson was a little disappointed because Phoumano was not bitten. "At least he could have had a heart attack!" However, the Laotian did lose face, and the business got off to a bad start, and the coffee was pretty good.

All in all, it was a good day's work!

Wilson and Trimmer returned from Khon Khen with good news. They'd met a Frenchman, Christian Nicholas, an employee of ESSO, who was willing to let them use his teletype and commu-nication system in his base station. The ESSO plant was relatively secure because the Thais seldom came inside the compound. This would give them a secure RTT (radio teletype and telephone) to the United States, and a phone and radio connections with Nakhon Phanom (NKP). Meanwhile, Loh had offered the use of his house

in NKP for another radio station. Under the latest plan, NKP was
to be their launch site.

Now they needed to move their equipment from Phoumi
Nosavon's bungalow. Gritz decided to make it a snatch operation.
Elaborate plans were made. The Americans rented two vans and
rehearsed their plan several times. However, the snatch was easier
than anticipated. When the time came, the guard waved them
through the compound gate. They casually loaded their equipment and drove back out. No questions were asked.

They left two men behind to make their presence felt in Bangkok and the remainder of the team moved to Khon Khen. From
there, they began ferrying men and equipment to NKP on the
overnight bus.

★ ★ ★

They found Loh Tharaphant to be a dynamic, dedicated man
willing to commit everything to his fight against Communism. Loh
had worked for 10 years with U.S. Air Force intelligence, providing information on enemy border-crossing activity for the protection of the U.S. airbase at Udorn. Loh was born in Hanoi, Vietnam,
but was now a Thai citizen. He owns a trucking company and is a
wealthy man, by anybody's standards. He is the Thai representative for the Vietnam Liberation Front headquartered in Paris.
This organization is dedicated to liberating Vietnam from the
Communists (page 81). Loh runs an underground railroad that has
been smuggling people and material in and out of Laos for 20
years. To manage his underground system he has established a
broad network of agents and close contact with Free Lao guerrillas
throughout Laos.

Shortly after their arrival in NKP, Loh produced a thick folder of
agent reports concerning American POWs and enemy activity in
Central Laos. Patterson and Loh set about translating the material
(verbatim translation):

AGENT REPORT ONE:

FROM: MR. SRI-KUAN (who is in troops that deliver food
to prison camps)

DATE: September 22, 1982

American pilots in Phoo-Soon (Phu Xun) prison, Cha-Phole, Province. There were about 300 American prisoners. But now there are about 120 prisoners been there and about 180 prisoners were sent to Do Ban Thoun. The job of prisoners are repair of the broken planes. Food: They have flesh of fish two time for a day and rice.

VIETNAM REGULARS:

There are about 108 Vietnam soldiers live at Phoo-Soon.

THE WATCHING:

There are four positions. There are watch tower all positions.

ENTRANCE:

Of prison are the cave that high about 2.5 meters.

★　　★　　★　　★　　★　　★　　★

AGENT REPORT TWO:

FROM: KHAM PHEU

DATE: 20 Oct 1982

8 U.S. POWs wearing VC green uniforms at Plei Ho Bo, 30 km from VN/Laos border in VN. Camp is open to aerial photo. All POW are pilots captured 65-70. POWs plant legumes—6 VC guards there three years.

★　　★　　★　　★　　★　　★　　★

AGENT REPORT THREE:

FROM: KHEIN LO BRUN

DATE: September 1982

The prison in Phoo-Soon between Chay-Phole Province (Lao) and Lao Bao (Vietnam). There were 300 American prisoner before after receive news that White Lao (non-Communists) soldiers will attack then Communists move 200

American prisoners to Ban Me Thuet. These American prisoners learn Vietnamese language every day by Vietnamese teacher.
- Guard ????? has 1 soldiers that will change every hour.
- There were about 100 Vietnam and Red Lao soldiers.
- There was a tank model T 65 still over there.
- The commandant of this prison is captain Sri-Khan.
- Plenty of food and drink. They have rice.

★　　★　　★　　★　　★　　★　　★

AGENT REPORT FOUR:

FROM: PHAY VAN SENG MA NE

There are 2 U.S. POWs alive and being held in Khan Khuet, learning Vietnamese from a Lao instructor.

★　　★　　★　　★　　★　　★　　★

AGENT REPORT FIVE:

FROM: NGHO PHU

DATE: 11 Nov. 1981

- Cuba engineers and Russian troops now control radar building at Ban Ta-Kong.
- At Ba Khaeng-kok had Russian troops about 80 persons.
- 20 American prisoners at the prison in Dak Tom Vietnam. The prison very dirty. They only eat (not able to translate)

★　　★　　★　　★　　★　　★　　★

AGENT REPORT SIX:

FROM NGUYEN VAN KINH, FREE LAO CHIEF AS REPORTED BY (CENSORED) WHO WORKS AT SENO AIRBASE IN LAOS.

- Seno has jet airfield with MIG 17, 19 from Vietnam also 3 C-130 aircraft; Russian Hind and OH-58 U.S. helicopters.

PLEDGE

The Revolutionary Front for Reconquest of Vietnam

Firmly believing in the traditionally tremendous courage of the people, in the perennial survival of the race and the glorious future of the nation;

Considering the fact that the Northern Vietnamese Communists, who are occupying the soil of Southern Vietnam, are operating as delegates and agents of foreigners and enemies, i.e. the USSR;

THE REVOLUTIONARY FRONT FOR RECONQUEST OF VIETNAM established by and composed of genuine Vietnamese patriots

— is determined to reconquer territorial sovereignty and free all the Vietnamese fellow-countrymen - from South to North - from the inhuman yoke of the HANOI dictatorship, so as to ensure real Peace, Freedom, Happiness and independence for all the Vietnamese people;

— is willing to co-operate with other nations in setting up and defending peace and liberty in Indo-China and elsewhere in the world.

I- POSITIONS
— To save the Nation is the supreme Law for everyone. Everything should be undertaken with a view to serve the people first;

— The dictatorial power of HANOI is the main enemy to be destroyed. Whosoever fights against HANOI may be considered as a friend and an ally;

— VIETNAM is an independent country within regional and world community, dealing with other countries on the basis of mutual respect regarding equality and sovereignty;

— All our endeavors aim at promoting a Vietnamese régime based upon Humanism, thus offering all necessary guarantees concerning Democracy and Freedom.

II- RECOMMENDATIONS
a) Territorial Reconquest

— The struggle in view of reconquering the national territory is the common duty for all the citizens: it should be persisting, continual and complete;

— The main strength in this fight dwells in the hands and the will of our people. Nevertheless, all friendly nations may be considered as a strong and necessary support movement.

b) Reconstruction and Renewal

To build up a renewed VIETNAM based on the following principles:
— Freedom, Democracy, Humanism
— Love, Equality, Reciprocity
— Culture: Tradition allied to Modernism
— Respect of private property according to the principle: «unity within community».

III- WAYS AND MEANS
— All national forces should be united into a powerful movement
— Our people are the natural allies of CAMBODIA and LAOS
— We are striving to secure international support on behalf of our National Cause

As a matter of fact, the HANOI Communist leaders, as acting delegates of expansionist USSR, are considered in the country as national traitors, and outside Vietnam as perfidious enemies of world peace. The HANOI dictatorship is definitely condemned to be overthrown.

THE REVOLUTIONARY FRONT FOR RECONQUEST OF VIETNAM, working for a noble Cause in conformity with all National ideals, feels absolutely sure to succeed in its endeavors aiming at National Reconquest and Reconstruction.

VIETNAM, June 20th, 1977

THE REVOLUTIONARY FRONT FOR RECONQUEST OF VIETNAM

Figure 11

VC battalion (500 men). VC Regiment 275 3,000 men now at
Mahaxay.
- VC 968 Division Headquarters at Ban Nong Xa.
- VC 384 Construction BN at Sepone (Phoo Soon) for road
bridge building.
- Muong Phin has jet runway for MIG aircraft. There are
now 40 Russian and Mongolians construction tech reps now
at Muong Phin for building large bridge between Muong
Phin and Sepone.
- At Seno have 122 rockets pointed toward east.
- At Savannakhet Khai Dong military station there are special weapons supplied by USSR stored in bunker protected
by wire and guard. Bunker is 2 m. deep in underground—3
steel doors. Pathet Lao Colonel told Chinese friends to leave
Nakhon Phanom area since weapons would destroy area between two points. Planned for war use. All communists will
pull out of area before use. Must use weapons only in dry
season because winds have east blow.
- One year ago VC defector said 30 U.S. POWs wearing blue
uniforms were used to maintain an aerial tram between two
mountains at Phu Xun.

★　　★　　★　　★　　★　　★　　★

A few days after the team's arrival in NKP, Loh introduced one
of his top agents to Gritz and Patterson. Mr. Sri-Kuan lived in
Savannakhet, Laos and worked for the Communists. Actually
Savannakhet is just across the Thai border (page 66). The agent
said that every two weeks he drove a truck delivering food to the
prison camp at Sepone near Phu Xun (Phoo-Soon) mountain. He
claimed that there were 100 Americans and two Frenchmen in
the camp. "The two Frenchmen are left unguarded because their
minds are gone." He said the prisoners were kept in a cave complex at night and brought out during the day to work in the fields
and attend class. He described the compound outside of the caves
as having one large building and one small. There was a Russian
T-65 tank at the front gate but he never saw it moved or manned.
Sri-Kuan said that he once talked to an American and asked him
to come with him. He promised the prisoner he would smuggle

83

him to Savannakhet in his truck, then help him to get to Thailand. The American broke down and cried, "We would never make it!"

Patterson suddenly found himself choked up. There were tears in his eyes and one rolled down his cheek. He wiped it off with the back of his hand. The agent sounded like he was telling the truth and his information backed up other evidence they had received on Sepone. It also coincided with the information supplied earlier by Phoumi Nosavon and General Vang Pao.

Sri-Kuan surprised them with his next statement.

"There is a secret weapon in Savannakhet that is pointed toward Nakhon Phanom."

"Do you know what kind of weapon it is?" asked Gritz.

"No, but I know it will kill every man, woman and child between Savannakhet and Nakhon Phanom. But it can't be fired during the rainy season because the winds blow to the East instead of toward Thailand."

"I have an agent report about this secret weapon," announced Patterson. He shuffled through a pile of papers until he found it. Both he and Gritz studied it.

"Do you think it's a nuke?" asked Patterson.

"No. It has to be a large rocket filled with a chemical agent—probably nerve gas or yellow rain," answered Gritz. All of the Free Lao guerrillas were terrified of yellow rain. They told tales of "whole villages being wiped out." According to the Free Lao, the chemicals were dispersed by airplane, artillery or rockets.

Gritz asked Sri-Kuan if he could hook him up to the small box. "It will tell whether or not you are telling the truth."

The agent agreed to be attached to the polygraph machine and Gritz proceeded to ask him questions pertaining to his story that required only a "yes" or "no" answer. The slowly moving needle on the lie detector graph hardly wavered in its journey. The machine said clearly "this man is telling the truth!"

The five Free Lao guerrilla chiefs that Loh had sent runners for finally arrived at NKP. One of them, Akhein, walked 160 miles to meet the Americans. Gritz and Patterson questioned and polygraphed each chieftan. Gritz did the questioning, Loh trans-

lated, and Patterson listened to ensure that the translation was correct. First they sat down and talked to each man to establish a good rapport. Then Gritz asked a series of questions pertaining to U.S. POWs:
- Have you seen American POWs?
- When did you see them?
- Where did you see them?
- How many did you see?
- What was their physical condition?
- What were they wearing?
- How many guards were at the prison?

Then the chief was hooked up to the polygraph and Gritz rephrased the questions based on the earlier answers so they required only a "yes" or "no" answer:
- Have you seen American POWs?
- Did you see them recently, or on or about _____?
- Did you see them at _____?
- Did you see about _____?
- Was their physical condition good?
- Were they wearing _____ uniforms?
- Were there _____ number of guards?

All but one of the chiefs (the one nearest to the Thai border) said they had seen American POWs within the last six months! Patterson felt the likable Akhein was the one who provided the best information. His village was only a few miles from Sepone and he claimed to have been in an American Strike Force during the war.

GRITZ: Have you seen any American POWs?

AKHEIN: YES. I SEE THEM ALMOST EVERY DAY.

GRITZ: Where did you see them?

AKHEIN: I SEE THEM NEAR SEPONE AT PHU XUN MOUNTAIN. THEY SLEEP CAVE AT NIGHT BUT COME OUT DURING DAY TO TEND GARDENS.

GRITZ: How many Americans did you see?

AKHEIN: I COUNT 100 AMERICANS AND TWO FRENCHMEN.

GRITZ: What is their physical condition?

AKHEIN: THEY SEEM IN GOOD CONDITION. SOME ARE CRIPPLE. SOME ARE IN LEADERSHIP

POSITIONS. YOU CAN TELL WHEN THEY TALK
EVERYBODY ELSE LISTENS.

GRITZ: What type of clothing are they wearing?

AKHEIN: SOME HAVE BLACK CLOTHES. SOME WEAR
FATIGUES AND SOME HAVE GRAY UNIFORMS.

Akhein drew a map showing the camp location (see page 86) and a map of the camp (see page 87). He said he never saw anyone on the tank. "Some guards sleep in caves at night with the prisoners while some go to sleep at the nearby villages. Most of the guards are Pathet Lao (Laotian Communists), but there is a small contingent of Vietnamese advisors. There are a few Russians and Cubans in the area but they are working on the bridge."

Akhein also related a story how he had unsuccessfully tried to get one of the American prisoners at Sepone to walk out with him: "The American began crying and said, 'No, the other one tried and he gave up.' "

He evidently was referring to the story the team had picked up from other sources that "sometime in 1981, one of the Americans escaped from Sepone and ran 160 miles barefoot through the jungle. He finally gave up less than 20 miles from the Thai border. His feet were in such bad condition, he couldn't walk any further. The Communists took him back to Sepone."

By this time, Patterson was so overwhelmed with emotion that he had to leave the room. He walked outside and looked up at the stars hovering close to the ground. It was an amazingly beautiful tropic night. The stars appeared so close that he felt as if he could reach up and pluck one out of the sky. They seemed to twinkle brighter as he watched them—as if they were laughing at him. Maybe they were. Maybe they knew something he didn't.

"Good God! Am I hearing what I'm hearing?" he asked himself aloud. "How can it be true? How could we, as a nation, just go off and leave these guys? How could we abandon them to such a fate? How could we leave them there to die in enemy hands? It would piss me off to think that one of my sons was left over there to live the rest of his life in a cave, living on a meager diet of rice and fish, treated no better than a wild animal. What if it was me over there in that cave? Could I have survived this long? And if I was still alive, what would I think of my country—the land of the free and the home of the brave?"

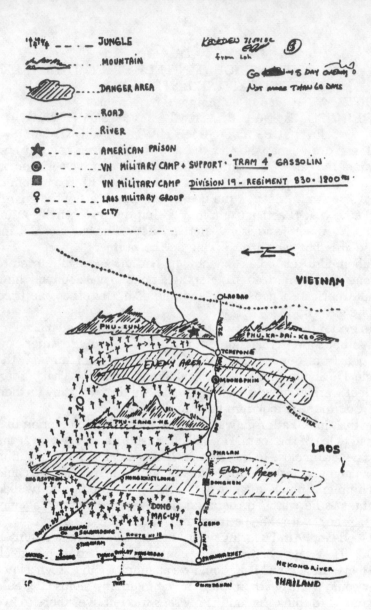

Figure 12
Map drawn by Akhein showing location
of POW camp near Sepone (Tchepone), Laos.

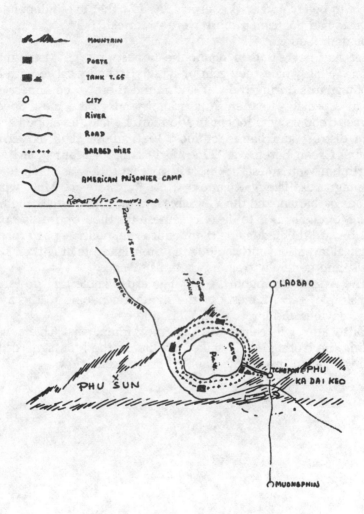

Figure 13
*Akhein's sketch of American POW camp
near Sepone (Tchepone), Laos.*

There was no longer any shred of doubt left in Patterson's mind. The American POWs were there. There was just too damn much proof to believe otherwise, especially now that five independent sources had confirmed there were American POWs at Phu Xun mountain (Sepone).

He had no reason to doubt the honesty of the Montagnard chiefs. What would they gain by lying? He had worked with the Montagnards during the war and found them to be honest and loyal, especially to their American friends. Like most Special Forces troopers who fought in Vietnam, he had developed a sincere distrust and hatred of most Vietnamese. The old saying among Green Berets was "One Yard (slang for Montagnard) was worth ten Vietnamese!" Some will say that ratio was unfair to the Montagnards. The Vietnamese word for them is "Moi" which means barbarian, and the Vietnamese treat them with contempt. The Montagnards hate the Vietnamese for their oppressive policies toward them: denying them education, political power, basic medical attention, and confiscating their land, stealing their livestock, and generally treating them as savages.

The Americans found the Montagnards likable and preferred the simple, naive honesty of the mountain people to the more wily, devious and inscrutable Vietnamese.

Patterson's gut-feeling was that the Montagnard Chiefs were telling the truth. He had staked his life on the Montagnards too many times in the past to doubt their sincerity now.

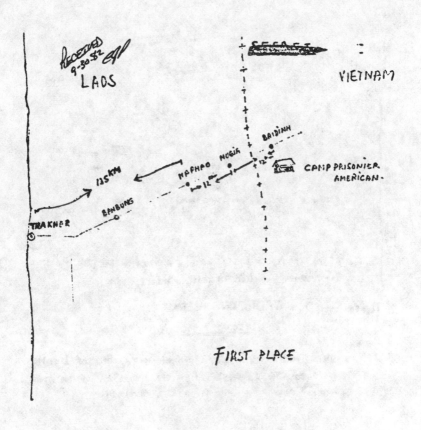

Figure 14
Map drawn by one of Loh's agents showing
location of American POW camp in Vietnam.

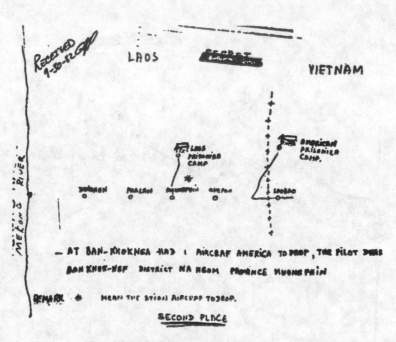

Figure 15
Intelligence report and map
turned in by one of Loh's agents.

*Men ejecting from flaming, exploding
aircraft, under missile fire, parachuting into
hostile territory; yet not one of those men
returned to us was missing an eye, ear, arm, leg
or finger, and none was disfigured by burns.
Obviously, several of our missing 2,500 POW/
MIAs must have been maimed during capture
or during interrogation. Might not Vietnamese
paranoia prevent them from repatriating those
who had been maimed?*

REHYANSKI, JOSEPH A.
"We Can Keep You Forever"
National Review, August 1981

CHAPTER TEN

The five guerrilla chiefs each agreed to furnish 100 armed men
and place them under Gritz's command for the rescue mission. In
return, they asked only for medical supplies and some food for
their people. As an added bonus, Gritz offered to give them all of
the Americans' equipment except the IDT boxes after the operation.

This started an American buying spree in Thailand. First, they
bought out all of the pharmacies in Nakhon Phanom, then they
started in on Bangkok.

**AUTHOR'S NOTE: It is rather difficult to maintain a low
profile when a husky bunch of Americans are running
around the country buying all the available medical supplies.**

**In Thailand, as in most countries in the Orient, the Middle
East and parts of Europe, antibiotics and other drugs can
be purchased in a pharmacy without a doctor's prescription. Some of the supplies were distributed to the refugee
camps; some were sent on ahead into Laos with men furnished by the chiefs, and the rest, the team planned to
carry in with them.**

★ ★ ★

On 1 November, the Team received a letter from Gordon Wilson who had returned to the United States:

BO:

1. Sent Cranston the message attached. Hope he will respond soon. Will advise.

2. Mr. Dick Salsburg is going to help some more when we get one of the sets of remains ID. I have told him we are having to pay $740 each for them and he agrees it is a shame but will contact other people in his area about contributing. We will do the best we can.

3. The LTC mentioned in the last message met Janet [Townley] in a bar and found she was an MIA daughter by the silver medallion she was wearing. He said he wanted to assure her there was definitely something going on and that he was involved. He said he had been in and out of Laos recently from the Special Forces group in Korea. He claims he knows Ramon. He also says there will be something in the media on the 24th of November. He says both overt and covert action is taking place at this time. His name is . . . Like you I wonder which side he is on. He talks too much. Jan will meet him again Monday.

4. I am staying in touch with Gritz and Clint both thru Ramon and direct contact. As soon as you have definite crossing time, we will activate and be on his plane to see the "Main Mugg" [President]. If support comes I will bring them to you. If not I will come to NKP with all the money and medical supplies I can find to wait your contact.

5. Maybe we should plan a diversion up north of your area just to get the heat off you in case you need it. I could bring some plastic in if Zap will tell me where to pick it up.

Hope to see you soon

God Bless you and all there

C.Y.A.

Gordon

Gritz and Patterson had decided that while they were in Thailand they would attempt to bring back the remains of any Americans that they could. They believed that if they had to pay $400 or $500 for the remains of one American, it would be worth the money. They put out the word through Loh's intelligence channels that the Americans were buying, if remains could be verified as Americans. During the first week of November, one set of bones were brought in by one of Loh's agents. The man claimed that he saw the American plane crash during the war and was forced by the Communists to bury the body of the pilot. He handed over to Gritz a skull, part of an arm bone and the hip bone.

AUTHOR'S NOTE: This is not the same set of bones Gritz brought back to the States with him in February 1983, which the government claimed were Oriental. According to Patterson, they never received any feedback from this first set of remains.

Gordon Wilson was due back from the U.S. but he was delayed, so Bill Batchelor came in his place. Patterson, who once served on the JCRC, gave the remains and a letter of introduction to Batchelor who flew to Hawaii and turned the remains over to the JCRC. The Laotian who brought the bones was never paid because Patterson told him he would be paid as soon as the bones were verified as being American.

Gordon Wilson was supposed to bring back three things that the Ground Team needed for the mission into Laos: maps of the first 65 miles; a hand-cranked generator (so they wouldn't have to carry so many extra batteries); and 9mm ammunition for the UZI's. When Batchelor arrived in Wilson's stead, all he had was the ammunition. Most of it was no good because it had been hand-loaded by Claudia Gritz and Ramon Rodcriguiz. Batchelor, who had easy access to the needed maps in Washington, said that Wilson didn't mention anything about the maps or hand-cranked generator. It appeared that at least some of Bo's bad luck was still traveling with him.

On 6 November, Claudia called her husband and notified him that the FBI was looking for him. They had come to the house and asked her where Bo was and what was he doing. They hinted that

he might be doing something that violated the neutrality act and could possibly be facing a prison sentence. It was evident that they had scared her half to death. Gritz had a few not-so-kind words to say about the friendly FBI.

In addition to the maps, generator, and ammunition, Wilson was also supposed to bring back an unbiased polygraph operator. Gritz wanted Loh to take a lie detector test. The results were to be shown to the President. He believed that if he could show Reagan that the primary source of their intelligence was telling the truth, then the President would be more likely to provide them with support. Now, things were changed. Since Wilson would not arrive before the mission was launched, the polygraph test would have to be delayed until after the meeting with the President.

Gordon Wilson had remained in the United States to make contact with Clint Eastwood and the President. The actor was supposed to set up a meeting with Reagan on the 27th of November at the President's ranch near Santa Barbara, while the President was there celebrating the Thanksgiving holidays. During the meeting, Wilson and Eastwood were to tell the President that Gritz and his team had crossed the border into Laos and were going to attempt to rescue American POWs.

On 7 November, the Team received a coded message from Wilson:

"MEETING SET WITH CLINT AND THE PRESIDENT STOP HURRY AND GET OVER STOP"

During the final days of preparation, Gritz and Patterson worked on an Intelligence Summary and Situation Report:

OPERATION LAZARUS

A. INTRODUCTION: This summary is compiled with the expressed intent of providing those persons with a need-to-know, an overview of the personalities, places and events within Southeast Asia comprising the current effort to resolve the POW/MIA issue evolving from the Vietnam War. *Operation Lazarus* is designed specifically to liberate U.S. POWs held captive against their will by Communist forces in

Southeast Asia and to return remains of those MIAs that become available for identification. This multi-faceted mosaic, when collectively pieced together, knits a coherent blueprint for accomplishing this bold and ambitious plan.

Intelligence has been gathered which pinpoints POW locations; targets have been selected based upon vulnerability, accessibility and chance of success; the U.S. team selection was based upon availability, willingness to commit, and experience; indigenous assets were filtered through a maze of test-challenges to weed out those with low potential. The results focus upon three distinct areas of effort: The primary is the liberation of U.S. POWs using Free Lao and Free Vietnamese Forces guided by a small U.S. Ground Tactical Team, led by Bo Gritz, who is also overall operation commander. The second effort is a finesse of U.S. POWs using Pathet Lao contacts to turn over Americans in return for sanctuary and/or rewards. The third effort seeks identifiable U.S. MIA remains from all sources.

This summary shall explore each of the areas identified so the reader may understand who, what, where, when, why and—most importantly—how *Operation Lazarus* can succeed.

B. ASSUMPTIONS: It is assumed, due to delicate diplomatic relations between the United States, Thailand and Laos, the U.S. Government (U.S.G.) cannot commit official assets until positive proof of U.S. POW presence is provided. It is assumed, once such a determination has been made, the U.S. Government will follow the President's stated policy to do whatever is required to return the POWs to U.S. control. The Thai Government can only look the other way due to their policy of providing sanctuary for Free Lao, Vietnamese and Cambodian forces, while appeasing their Communist neighbors by not directly supporting guerrilla activity access to the Thai border.

It is assumed the Free Guerrilla Forces can approach POW locations and access them by force, if desired. It is also assumed that the underground auxiliary forces are adequate to support such a tactical operation and act as an evasion mechanism, should aerial support be denied in evacuating POWs to safety once liberated.

It is assumed the U.S.G. will tacitly allow the operation. Careful planning has blended high technology, special operations experience and audacity with existing unconventional warfare potential in the local area into a precision, intensive mission that can succeed if properly supported.

Finally, it is assumed that once liberation has been accomplished, the U.S.G. will follow up with strong, positive initiatives that will resolve the POW/MIA issue with a final and accurate accounting. It is hoped that the U.S.G. will also continue to support clandestinely those dedicated indigenous troops that made the liberation possible.

C. U.S. POW SITUATION: There appear to be several hundred live American POWs scattered throughout multiple locations along the Laos-Vietnam border within a target belt approximately 150 miles long by 100 miles wide. Geographically, the majority of U.S. POWs are located from Xieng Kon in the north to Saparon in the south. All are located along a major supply route or major routes of communication between Vietnam and Laos. The largest faction confirmed through numerous cross-checking is located at three closely positioned sites in the Sepone area. One camp at Phu Xun mountain has 100 Americans, as reported by a Lao with access to the camp, a mountain guerrilla chief and two other sources with either firsthand or secondary knowledge. A second area has 35 Americans, while the third has 5 Americans along with over 1,000 Free Lao and Vietnamese prisoners.

The POWs are reportedly in good physical health and performing time-passing tasks such as gardening, teaching English to Lao Communists, learning Lao and Vietnamese, and helping with general maintenance of facilities. While security is considerable in terms of manpower and material, the POWs are allowed contact with the local population. The guard force is primarily Pathet Lao, who live with their families near the POW camps.

D. KEY INDIGENOUS PERSONALITIES

1. General Phoumi Nosavon: Former Deputy Premier under UN Tri-parliament of Laos, who currently resides in Bangkok. Has a shadow government sketched out, but little key support from Thai officials. Has four military regions planned with small groups of refugee Lao residing in Thai camps to someday expand and occupy them. Requested a one billion dollar loan from Arab-backed U.S. lenders; the loan is not likely to go through, as there is a dearth of collateral. Overall, Phoumi does have loyal right-wing groups along the Lao-Thai border that support him and several isolated military strongholds within Laos, but he is an old and selfish fat man with little direct influence with the Thais and Lao. Understands most English.

2. Phoumano Nosavon: Son of Phoumi; a former C-47, T-28 pilot trained in the U.S. Phoumano works for a French news service and lives with his father in Bangkok. When given money to support the rescue mission, he pocketed it and lied to his father about the

amount. General Phoumi made the comment that his son was a thief and does not represent him. Phoumano is even more selfish and devious than his father.

3. Capt. Akhein: Loh-oriented mountain guerrilla leader from the Sepone area and has no knowledge of the terrain between the Mekong River and Highway 13. He has local support and village stronghold in the Phu Xun area. Because he reportedly killed seven Kham Bou neutralists this year, he is aggressively sought by Kham Bou and fears him.

4. General Kham Bou: A self-made general subordinate to General Khong Le who, as a young paratroop captain, overthrew the UN Tri-parliament in favor of neutralism. Kham Bou must reside inside Laos since making a public news statement that it was his aim to retake 17 provinces back from Thailand for Laos. Kham Bou appears to have a larger following than Phoumi, probably because he is closer to the Lao people. His stronghold encircles the Khum Maun area which is tightly patrolled against VC, PL and Phoumi forces. Kham Bou has indicated support for our operation since it will deal the Communists a severe blow and might result in aid for his forces. His mentor, General Khong Le, a world traveler, is now negotiating with both the Chinese Reds and Americans for support. Kham Bou appears to be the single most powerful Lao residing in the Far East.

5. Capt. Kham An: Crossing master for all official Free Lao in the area. He does not go into Laos himself but has control over sizeable paramilitary forces commanded by LT Ban Thom. He fears Kham Bou and responds to his requests for help.

6. Lt. Ban Thom: chief subordinate of Kham An. A strong, intelligent, capable leader. He lives in Thailand with Kham An but ventures into Laos and knows General Kham Bou. He has his own guerrilla warfare operating area in Bu Thou to Kon Thiep area.

7. Capt. Kham Sing: Subordinate to General Kham Bou who is dependent upon Lt. Ban Thom for river crossings. Kham Sing has details on the POW camp at Phu Xun to include the commander's name and various staff and job assignments. He is familiar with the Phu Xun area and has identified 48 supportive villages that will provide information, food and protection from Communist forces. Kham Sing is an Americanized Lao with good looks and a strong dedication to Kham Bou.

8. Capt. Bou Thet: An aggressive Kham Bou guerrilla leader. He has a relative who is Pathet Lao and assigned to a POW camp. Bou Thet

destroyed a bridge along Highway 9 in October 1982, and has initiated several contacts with the Communists which have accounted for over 20 KIA (killed in action). He has 80 armed men. He sent a runner to the U.S. team with a message that he would be waiting for us until 5 January 1983, and then return to Thailand. He, along with Akhein, Kham Sing and one other Lao, confirms the three POW locations at Scpone.

From the brief descriptions above, it should be readily apparent why the Communists occupy Laos. The Free Lao forces are so divided over personality differences that they will not marshal their forces against a common enemy. Phoumi is a cheat who receives money from U.S. Lao to care for his people in refugee camps along the border of which little, if any, arrives at the camps. General Vang Pao, Highlands leader of Military Region II, now lives in Montana, USA and coordinates the United Lao Development Corporation in the U.S. He has not set foot into Thailand or Laos since 1975. General Khong Le is highly respected but, like the others, prefers to live apart from his people. Only General Kham Bou, by his own undoing, is forced to live in the interior of Laos.

More so now than ever before, the Thais are currently tightening their grip on Free Lao movement across the border. After registration of all forces in Thailand, no further Lao shall be permitted to enter. The Thais make a practice of confiscating weapons and munitions that come into the country from Laos.

The villages in Laos support the Free Lao passively, if not openly. The people dislike the Vietnamese occupation as it draws heavily upon their always-short resources, and represses their religious practices. There is no shortage of manpower—only hardware and guidance.

With a minimum effort on the part of the U.S.G., a sizeable Free Lao military force could be developed that would require Vietnam to split its Cambodian-oriented forces or be forced to withdraw from Laos. It could provide a land bridge for insertion of Free Vietnamese forces that want to return home and fight the Communists. A force-multiplier provided by high technology and training could span the difference between Free Lao personalities and knit them into a tight weave that might not work together, but would coordinate with Americans toward a liberated Laos.

Black or gray operations are not difficult, using contract-type arrangements with reliable personnel. The liberation of U.S. POWs will deal a heavy blow to the Communists and focus world attention upon Laos; it should not wane before seeing Free Lao forces taking the initiative against the Vietnamese.

E. CONCEPT OF OPERATIONS:

1. Recovery and Identification of Remains:

Receive from any source, remains that have supporting information, such as dog tags, ID cards, tail numbers, crash sites, etc., for shipment to the JCRC ID Lab in Hawaii. Initial expenses will be paid up to a maximum of 2,000 Bhat, until positive ID is established, then a bonus of 8,000 Bhat, for a total of 10,000 Bhat ($444 U.S.).

While it is distasteful to buy back our dead—and in many cases the remains of Asians—$444 is a small price to pay in order to resolve an MIA family's anguish regarding the fate of their loved one.

2. Finesse of U.S. POWs:

There are three reports regarding instances where U.S. POWs have been approached by Free Lao and asked if they would like to return to the USA. In one case, it was attempted unsuccessfully; in two instances the Americans refused because they didn't think it possible. In each case, the Americans showed strong emotions in wanting to be returned.

Phoumi has contact with Pathet Lao authorities that have access to prisoners (from six to eight) that could be brought to the Thai border and turned over. Phoumi reportedly dispatched an agent to arrange just such a transfer. The Pathet Lao would require either sanctuary, should the transfer become public knowledge, or remuneration for their effort. Capt. Khuan Long has access to five POWs through a Pathet Lao. It is possible that these men could be freed through finesse at the same time a forced liberation was being initiated at Phu Xun.

All avenues of finesse should be explored and worked in conjunction with the forced liberation. Failing actual freeing of U.S. POWs through finesse, the ID and intelligence numbers and locations can be used later in negotiations to resolve the POW issue.

3. Forced Liberation:

A small U.S. team, led by Bo Gritz, crosses the Mekong River with an armed contingent of Free Lao en route to Nhoung Khiet Long in liaison with General Kham Bou. Five area chiefs have pledged support for the operation. How much actual armed support will be forthcoming remains to be seen, but 100 men from each area, plus initial crossers of the Mekong River, would provide a sizeable force that could forcefully free POWs from Phu Xun. If it appears feasible, a coordinated effort might be made to hit all three locations simultaneously. The POWs would then be withdrawn back through a protective village net as rapidly as possible, while Free Lao Forces provide diversionary action to cover the movement. Those POWs unable to move to prepared landing zones for airlift to U.S. control could be secured in stay-behind locations provided by Free Lao auxiliary forces and village support. Airlift could best be accomplished through NKP Air Base and coordination with Thais. Considering the path of flight will parallel two MIG bases (Seno and Savannakhet), either Thai or U.S. Navy fighter cap over the border would be advised. Straight line distance to Sepone is 125 miles. Helicopter turn-around would probably be two and one-half to three hours. Without either pre-strike or fighter cap, the lift birds will be extremely vulnerable to attack by MIG, HIND, and AA. If no vertical lift is available, the POWs will be moved or left behind through a chain of friendly villages (a total of 25 friendly villages have been identified near the NKP to Sepone route). The Mekong is one mile wide with a very strong current. POWs could not be expected to swim the distance. To remain on the far bank for any length of time will invite massing of Communist forces and recapture. The POWs can probably be freed from any one location with a 60% chance of success. Multiple rescues reduce success ratio by 20%. If no assistance from outside is given, 10% of those freed can be expected to survive the movement to the Mekong and subsequent unsupported crossing.

4. Alternatives:

If the Executive Branch has a better plan for freeing U.S. POWs, that plan should be made known ASAP (as soon as possible) to the field team so that proper support can be rendered. The team can provide photographs, locations, numbers, enemy, weather, terrain data, LZ-DZ (landing zone-drop zone) information, pathfinder operation in support of U.S. ground effort, route control, diversion, stay behind, underground operations, attack and control of limited objective hard points, guides, infiltration-exfiltration overland, target assessment and other on-order type missions. The purpose of *Operation Lazarus* is to liberate U.S. personnel being held against their will by the Communists, not to increase the number of POWs. While bold, the plan of attack has been carefully balanced around the calculated risk. The risk is high, but if success was not equally high, we would not risk our freedom and embarrassment to our country. *Operation Lazarus* will work if the U.S. Government will commit itself to rescuing U.S. warriors with the same zeal they were committed during the Vietnam war. Facing truth and reality will find the U.S. emerging a stronger nation while showing our military that they are a part of our society, not apart from it. The POWs served and fought while others dodged and were granted amnesty. We have embraced those who failed to go—let us now provide a final embrace for those we left behind and save them from the despicable fate of dying alone in the hands of our enemies.

F. SUMMARY: This overview should be combined with all of the intelligence reports and situation summaries generated during the past three months of *Operation Lazarus*. The operation is not simplistic in its approach to freeing U.S. POWs and should not be lightly dismissed as an amateur effort to do what is best left to professionals. The Commander has extensive experience planning and conducting unconventional operations of this nature and has served in key positions on both the Army Staff and Office of the Secretary of Defense. There is an acute appreciation for both the political and public sensitivity as well as the international ramifications involved. Having considered the entire scheme of players and possible results, it was decided to do whatever was required to bring an honorable and timely end to an issue that has dragged on without measurable progress for 12 years. Obviously, there must be a change in dynamics. Certain high level intelligence officials were sufficiently concerned about the issue to allow unofficial efforts through the private sector. General Tighe sawed off the limb behind him at retirement by stating in his personal assessment that we had left POWs behind. Now the President, the NSC Advisor, and the Secretary of Defense have all lamented that there are servicemen alive and in captivity.

It was not my original intention to involve myself with something I had put behind me, but I was commissioned to verify the existence of U.S. POWs. I preferred to believe that there were none; it would have been more convenient, and I could have resumed my military career. Unfortunately, there are U.S. POWs still alive and, although fired from my position as private sector rep, as a human being I cannot abandon my comrades. Like it or not, the USA must deal with the situation, no matter how uncomfortable it may prove to be. I have total faith in my Commander-in-Chief, the President of the United States of America, but I also know that legions of faint hearts separate him from difficult issues. Careful steps have been taken to insure the gatekeepers do not shut this out, and that self-centered cynics do not get a chance to vote.

Those who join me bet their lives that America will measure up to its responsibility. It is time that the POWs come home. I intend to do everything within my power to accomplish that end by the close of the year. I do not believe the United States is my enemy. I intend to cooperate with Executive desires. The POW/MIA dilemma needs to be resolved. If I and my people don't do it, I don't know anyone in Washington who will. It takes action, and both Teddy Roosevelt and John Wayne are dead. Hopefully, like the name of this operation, their spirit and resolve lives today in the heart of our President, resurrected as those declared dead by our system, soon will be.

> JAMES G. "BO" GRITZ
> COMMANDER
> *OPERATION LAZARUS*

AUTHOR'S NOTE: To protect the cover of Free Lao who may still be operating across the Thai-Laos border, some names have been changed. Names of POW camps not exposed by *Operation Lazarus* have also been changed.

★   ★   ★

AUTHOR'S NOTE: Gritz assumes in his Intelligence Summary and Situation Report that the U.S. Government will act quickly and come to his aid once he has freed American POWs and has them in hand, and provide an extraction airlift and necessary support to extract the rescue team and freed POWs out of Laos. In all probability, he is correct in assuming that President Reagan would act aggressively to bring the POWs out, provided the President had indisputable evidence that prisoners had been rescued. However, the arrangement set up by Gritz (Eastwood to the President) was "iffy" at best—radio from Laos to Thailand, phone to Los Angeles, phone to Eastwood, then Eastwood to the President—still only provides the President with third-hand information. He could not act without further proof.

A surprise raid by U.S. Government forces with all assets on hand (helicopters for extraction, escort and support aircraft, troops, etc.) is one thing; an unsupported raid by Gritz's team, where assets for extraction would have been martialed after-the-fact, is another. Gritz's raid would

alert the Communists. If the U.S.G. decided to come to Gritz's aid it would have taken time—time enough also for the Communists to get ready. American casualties on an exfiltration where there was no element of surprise could be very high.

Gritz's assumptions concerning the Thai Government were also erroneous. There was no assurance that the Thais would (1) look the other way and, (2) come to the aid of Gritz's team at the request of the U.S.G. The Thai's position in SEA, with over 450,000 Communist troops poised along their border, ready to pounce at the slightest provocation, was extremely precarious. The domino theory has been working in Southeast Asia as the Communists have annexed South Vietnam, Laos and Cambodia. Thailand is the next domino. The Thais historically have tried to remain neutral, and their current active policy is one of appeasement of their Communist neighbors.

In his summary, Gritz makes an impassioned plea for the U.S. to support General Kham Bou, (whom he likens to Simon Bolivar), and again become involved in the hostilities in Southeast Asia. Although the idea has some merit because it might put pressure on the Vietnamese to account for our MIAs, the U.S. is not likely now, or in the near future, to provide assistance to the Free Lao forces. (However, before long we may provide some arms and equipment to the Cambodian rebels). With all the internal and inter-tribal conflicts in Laos, not even "Lawrence of Laos" could inspire the various factions to work together against the Communists.

In his summary, Gritz says that if he has to exfiltrate the rescued prisoners on foot, only 10 percent of the POWs would survive. In other words, if he rescues 100 Americans, he is willing to have 90 die on the trip out—a high price to pay for fame, pride and a ride down Fifth Avenue.

"Although the North Vietnamese denied at the time holding any prisoners of war, during the next two years (1954–1956) they turned over to the French command three groups of alleged ralliers totaling 380 men. During the 1960s and early 1970s the North Vietnamese released several hundred North African and well over 100 European Foreign Legionnaires—notably Spaniards and Italians—who were repatriated to their countries of origin.

ANITA C. LAUVE, Internationally known expert on POW/MIAs

CHAPTER ELEVEN

The final plan for *Operation Lazarus* called for the Ground Team (Gritz, Patterson, Zappone, and Goldman) to cross the Mekong on "X-day", vicinity of That Phanom, with an armed escort of 15 Free Lao, and proceed to the POW camp on Phu Xun mountain near Sepone, Laos. During the movement to the target area, they would rendezvous with five Free Lao guerrilla forces. On "D-day", Akhein, with a force of 100 men, would conduct a diversionary attack on Sepone and withdraw to the south drawing off a number of the guards. The main force, led by Gritz, would then attack from the north, take down the remainder of the guards, and liberate the American POWs. The main force would withdraw to a nearby landing zone where, it was hoped, they would be extracted by U.S.G. forces or Thai forces at the request of the U.S. Government. If outside support failed to develop, the main force would withdraw to Thailand with the rescued prisoners, through a series of friendly villages.

Gritz believed that he would eliminate outside interference and by-pass all U.S. intelligence channels by having Clint Eastwood contact the President directly. He was, in effect, planning to force the President's hand. He reasoned that when the President found out that Americans were already in Laos to find and free POWs, he would have no recourse but to order certain U.S.G. forces to prepare plans to come to the Team's rescue. Gordon Wilson, who would be with Eastwood, knew the details of the plan, so U.S.G. forces could make contingency plans based upon the "Intelligence Estimate and Summary," which was being hand-carried to the U.S. If the Team rescued POWs, the President would have to issue orders to U.S.G. forces to "act" in an all out effort to extract the Team and rescued prisoners from Laos to friendly territory. Gritz believed that when the U.S. had undisputed evidence of POWs in Vietnam and Laos, it would place pressure on Vietnam and obtain the release of the remainder of U.S. POWs.

In retrospect, considering President Reagan's decision to move into Grenada, Gritz was probably correct in his assumptions. Reagan would have sent forces into Laos to rescue the Team and any liberated American POWs, providing he had proof positive they existed.

The first crossing date was scheduled for 15 November. On the 15th, the Team received word that all the refugee camps were locked up. No one could get in or out. It seems the Thai Government chose this particular time to collect refugees' Food Ration Cards and issue new ones. They had to do this every few months. Because of a booming black market business in counterfeit ration cards, it had to be unannounced. In every country there are plenty of vultures who take advantage of the unfortunate people when money can be made. The mission was postponed until the 23rd.

On the 20th, the Team received its second message from Gordon Wilson concerning the meeting with the President. "MEETING STILL SET. MUST GO!" Wilson.

On the 23rd, they were again forced to postpone the crossing. This time, the Thais had some sort of border operation going on and there were military units all over the area. The Americans never did find out if it was just a practice alert or if something real was going on. One thing for sure, it was no time to try to sneak across the border.

On the 24th, Patterson received word from his wife that she hadn't received any money. Each Team member's family was supposed to receive $500 a week while they were in Thailand.

This money was [supposed] to come from donated monies being held by Larry Palma in Washington. Patterson was understandably concerned. The last few months without a job had put a severe financial strain on his family. His wife was working; however, she wasn't making enough to pay the family expenses. This $500 a week, which was only going to be paid while they were out of the U.S., was sorely needed at home.

Gritz picked up the phone and called his wife in L.A. She confirmed the bad news. She had not received any money either. Bo tried to call Palma that day, but was unable to reach him.

Gordon Wilson called on the 25th. When Gritz asked about the Team members' pay, Gordon said that over $27,000 had been collected in the fund raising. However, he claimed there was nothing left because Jack Bailey and retired Congressman Donald Bailey (no relation) had taken off with the money to Geneva, Switzerland.

Bo was livid! But what could he do? He wrote a letter to Larry Palma, in charge of East coast fund raising, which Patterson typed:

WE AREN'T IN ANY POSITION TO DO ANYTHING NOW—BUT IF WE LIVE TO GET BACK HOME ALIVE, A PAYBACK, WITH INTEREST, WILL BE FORTHWITH— AND PAYBACKS IN THIS BUSINESS ARE A MOTHER-FUCKER!

By the time the 27th rolled around (it was still the 26th in America), the Americans were getting nervous. This tense waiting period didn't seem to bother the Lao. They acted as if there was no sense of urgency—for them, there probably wasn't. Gritz knew they had to go tonight or never. The meeting with President Reagan was scheduled for the 27th. The Team had to be inside Laos when the meeting was held. First, because they didn't want Clint Eastwood lying to the President, and, second, once across the river, it would be too late for the U.S. Government to persuade the Thais to stop the mission.

"We're going across tonight, come hell or high water," Gritz declared positively.

The Team spent the day making final preparations: packing rucksacks, cleaning weapons, filling water canteens, sharpening knives, resting, and writing last minute letters home.

Patterson couldn't rest. He felt the old adrenaline pumping; excitement, the anticipation of the mission coming up. It was like old times. He was ready. He made a last check of his rucksack. He was carrying 15 days' rations, 15 extra radio batteries, one IDT box, two five-quart collapsible water containers, two sacks of medical supplies to distribute to the Free Lao, ten survival straws (These little babies are fantastic. They have built-in water purifiers —you can drink safely out of a recently used toilet!), four boxes of 9mm ammunition, spotter binoculars, a nylon fishnet hammock, poncho and poncho liner, garrotte saw, lensatic compass, extra socks, foot powder and a field dressing. The damned thing weighed over 150 pounds! In Vietnam, the average pack for a mission behind enemy lines weighed about 40 pounds. The individual loads were going to be heavy, all because Wilson had neglected to send the hand-cranked generator. Now, they had to pack enough extra radio batteries for the mission. Patterson wished to hell that Wilson was here to carry his pack.

Each American carried a laminated card with an American flag on it to be used in an emergency. It identified the bearer as an American and requested help in six languages: Thai, Laotian, Vietnamese, Cambodian, Chinese and English, with a reward offered to get back to American control (see page 109). It probably was a useless document to carry, but when you are operating behind enemy lines you try to give yourself every ounce of edge to survive.

Just prior to moving out to the launch site, Gritz held an awards ceremony. He pinned a U.S. Army Commendation Medal on Loh and read the certificate: "For providing outstanding assistance in gathering intelligence, etc." Loh and his family were devout Catholics and, after the awards ceremony, Gritz had them join hands while he prayed.

At this point Patterson left the area. He had given up on prayers several years ago. "When my son was dying, I prayed and prayed, but it didn't do any good."

The Americans loaded themselves and their equipment into Loh's pickup and drove to the launch site near the Pak Nam Ping

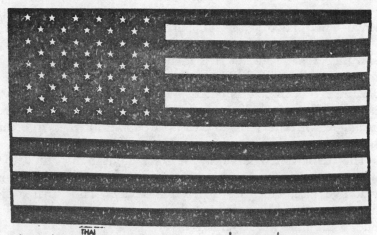

THAI

ข้าพเจ้าเป็นคนสัญชาติอเมริกัน ภูมภาษาของท่านไม่ได้
ขคร้าพเจ้าให้ข้าพเจ้าต้องการดความรวบเหลือจากท่านในเรื่อง อาหาร
ที่พัก และความคุ้มครอง โปรดพาข้าพเจ้าจนพบไปผู้ใดผู้หนึ่ง
สามารถจะให้ความปลอดภัยแก่ข้าพเจ้า และสาพางสังข้าพเจ้ากลับ
สถานเมืองระชะชาติขา้วกับย รัฐบาลของข้าพเจ้าจะตอบแทนใน
วามรวบเหลือของท่าน.

LAOTIAN

ສາມ ສິ່ເຄົາຣິບ

ຂ້າພະເຈົ້າ ເປັນຍງາເມຣິກັນ . ຂ້າພະເຈົ້າ ປາກພາຍາລາ
ວຽຄານຍໍ່ໄດ້ . ເຄາະຮ້າຍ ໄດ້ບັງຄັບໃສ່ ຂ້າພະເຈົ້າ ມາຫາ
ວາມຮວຍເສືອຈາກຫານ ຈະເປັນເຄື່ງກັນ ຜູ້ ໃສ່ສ່ຽວພາງາໂຍ
ໃສຫາມປຶກປັກຮັກຫາ ຢ່າງໃດກໍ່ດີ . ຈຶ່ງກະຣຸນາາ ຂ້າພະເຈົ້າ
ປສາຫຼ້າໃຫຍ່ບູ ຜື່ຍຈະໃຄຄວາມຍຄໄນ ເຂົາ້ພະເຈົ້າໄດ້ ແລະ
ະພຍາຍາຈັດຊື່ງ ຂ້າພະເຈົ້າ ກັບຄືນເມືອຫານັ້ນວຽະເນຣິກັນ .
ຄຸນາມຮງ ຂ້າພະເຈົ້າ ຈະຊົມຕະບາຍຄຸນຫານ.

ຂຍໃຈຫາຍາ ບຣິຫານຫັ່ຈະໄດ້ຈວຍເຫຼືອ .

CAMBODIAN

VIETNAMESE

Tôi là một người Mỹ. Tôi không nói được tiếng Việt. Cảnh bất hạnh
may rủi gặp nhủ, nay tôi phải cầu cứu đến. Làm hết. Cho tôi ăn uống và
bảo vệ tôi. Hãy đưa tôi cho một người nào có thể giúp cho sự an toàn và
cho tôi trở về với dân tộc tôi. Chính Phủ chúng tôi sẽ đền ơn tạ nghĩa ạ.

ENGLISH

I am a citizen of the United States of America. I do not speak your
language. Misfortune forces me to seek your assistance in obtaining food,
shelter and protection. Please take me to someone who will provide for my
safety and see that I am returned to my people. My government will
reward you.

Figure 16
Card carried by Lazarus team members in Laos.

canal, two miles south of That Phanom. The Free Lao followed in two vans. The armed escort was made up of Akhein—who was to leave to patrol two days in and journey on alone to pick up his men —and 14 men provided by Loh's agent, Captain Savoi, who was also the crossing master. His men regularly pulled intelligence missions in Laos for the Thais. They were issued weapons by the Thai Army for these excursions. When they returned, they had to turn the weapons back into the Thais. Supposedly, it had been arranged with the Thais to pick up weapons for this "intel" mission.

The Team waited nervously for Loh's agent to show up with the weapons. As they waited, they searched the far side with the night vision goggles, which were effective devices. They turned night into bright day. They could easily have spotted a man on the far side of the mile-wide Mekong River.

At 2300 hours, the agent showed up without the weapons. He excitedly explained to Loh that he was unable to get them because the Thai sergeant who had the keys was drunk.

The Americans were shocked, angry and extremely frustrated. Here they were "cocked and locked" and ready to go, and they had three UZIs and one .38 caliber pistol for 19 men. Patterson was too stunned to speak! The mission would have to be delayed again. He walked over and threw his rucksack back into the pickup.

Gritz was more determined. This was the moment he had aimed at for over four years! Nothing was going to stop him. "We can't back out now because Wilson meets with the President tomorrow. We've got to go tonight!" he declared.

Patterson looked unbelievingly at his boss. "Well, what do you want to do?"

Gritz picked up his pack and slung it across his shoulders. "It's a good night to die. Fuck it, let's go!"

Patterson felt an icy chill of fear run down his back. The first thought that ran through his mind was: "Hey! There's no damned night a good night to die." He turned to Gritz. "We can't go in with just three weapons. That would be stupid. Let Wilson lie to the President and we'll go in tomorrow night."

"No," returned Gritz. "We can't lie to the President. We go now!

We'll have plenty of security when we meet up with Kham Bou's men."

"That's over 65 miles away!" interjected Goldman.

"Okay, we'll sneak and peek until then," said Gritz. "Let's go!"

Patterson knew that Gritz had made up his mind. He was going, and he expected them to follow. No one could dissuade their leader now. He reached in the pickup, took out his rucksack and tossed it over his shoulder. With an "ah shit" under his breath, he followed Gritz.

They loaded into three sampans. Patterson was a little surprised that the Lao were willing to go unarmed, but they didn't seem to mind. "They run around over there all the time without weapons so they aren't too worried," said Loh. "Besides, they don't think you will run into any trouble before you meet Kham Bou."

One of the sampans had a motor and towed the other two across. The crossing was uneventful and once on the other side they unloaded hurriedly and moved across the 300 meters of open beach. Gritz directed the Americans to give their weapons to the point-and-flank security men. They moved south, parallel to the Mekong, until they reached a small tributary. Then they turned east, into Communist controlled territory. Patterson felt naked as a newborn babe without his weapon, but he figured Gritz's reasoning was correct. The security people should have the weapons. He still wasn't sure that they should have crossed the river without weapons, but the game was on. They were committed. He felt a little of the old exhilaration pumping through his body. Besides, it was a beautiful night—a good night for a hike in the country. But it sure as hell wasn't a good night to die!

From Vietnamese refugees have come scores of eyewitness accounts of groups of emaciated Americans, some in chains, being led under heavy guard through villages or along jungle trails to unknown destinations. Some of the firsthand sightings were reported as late as 1980, five years after the fall of Saigon and seven years after the return of 566 American POWs from Hanoi, supposedly the last of our survivors. It is noteworthy that 13 French prisoners captured at Dien Bien Phu were not released by Hanoi until 16 years later.

SINGLAUB, JOHN K.
Major General
U.S. Army, Retired
"Let's Find Our Missing Men"
The American Legion Magazine, 1980

CHAPTER TWELVE

LAOS, 28 NOVEMBER 1982

They walked single file through the dark jungle. The jungle was not dense here, and they alternated between patches of thick vegetation and open rice paddies. They moved with that strange forward stoop of men carrying heavy loads on their backs. The movement could best be described as a forward-leaning shuffle.

The straps of the heavy rucksack bit deeper into Patterson's shoulders with each step. They were carrying too much weight— far too much! "Damn that fucking Wilson!" he mumbled to himself. Rivulets of perspiration trickled down his face and dripped from his chin. Every few minutes he had to wipe the stinging sweat from his eyes. A strange feeling came over him—a feeling of having been here before, of having lived this moment before. He had, but in a different time and place. In a land called Nam. How many times had he done this before, in Vietnam? Countless! There, he was the classic "Green Beret Grunt," carrying a heavy load of equipment and ammunition; slogging through the rice paddies, elephant grass, and thick jungle; tripped and grabbed by the "gotcha vines"; eaten alive by swarms of mosquitoes; blood sucked out by leeches as big as your finger; looking, searching for the illusive enemy.

This time, things were different. He was not as young. He didn't want to find the enemy. Good God—not with only three weapons! And he wasn't on a mission to kill; he was on a mission of mercy.

Patterson looked ahead in the column at the broad shoulders of Bo Gritz. Bo wasn't an old man—but he was too damned old to be doing this kind of thing! The legendary Green Beret had changed in the last few weeks as the frustrations piled upon his obsession to rescue the prisoners. He almost seemed paranoid. The "old Gritz" would never have stepped off behind enemy lines with only three weapons for 19 men. Hell, he would have told their superiors to go fuck themselves! And then there was all that joking about his being "Lawrence of Laos"—or was Bo kidding? Patterson was beginning to wonder. He realized that Bo was under a lot of pressure. Bo had lived with this thing for four years—four years of meeting frustrations and setbacks at every turn, and finally being spurned by the U.S. Government. Only someone with Gritz's strength and determination could have carried on. It was a miracle Bo hadn't lost his senses by now.

Ah, hell, thought Patterson, Bo was Bo and he was still the best damned "special ops officer" around. If anyone could accomplish this mission, Bo could!

Patterson looked ahead. There was a slight red tinge on the horizon. The eastern sky was beginning to show the first signs of dawn. They would soon have to find a bivouac for the day, then he could get the damned rucksack off his back for awhile. This part of Laos reminded him of the area in Vietnam along the Cambodian border. Again, that feeling of deja vu came over him. It was just before dawn at an earlier time in another place, just like this:

TAY NINH PROVINCE, VIETNAM 1968

Patterson slowly parted the tall elephant grass with the barrel of his Swedish K submachine gun and looked across the small clearing ahead. It looked safe enough. It was quiet; even the night birds had stopped talking in the presence of his patrol. He shifted the weapon into his left hand and wiped the sweat from his brow with the back of his hand. He looked sinister with black camouflage paint streaked across his face, but the stuff was also a good mosquito repellant. The gray light of dawn was beginning in the east, and eerie shadows jumped and danced across the clearing. He shivered, not from the cold; it was just a feeling that ran down his back—a feeling that something was not quite right. This area was spooky as hell! He was commanding a 56-man Cambodian platoon on a search and destroy mission. The Communists had been hitting the Tri-Be Special Forces Camp for a week with mortars and ground-probing attacks. His job was to locate and destroy them. So far, this night, they had drawn a blank. God! He wanted a cigarette, bad! But he didn't dare take the chance. It would be light in a few minutes anyway. He removed one from the pack in his left breast pocket and stuck it, unlighted, into his mouth. He stood up slowly and signaled his point man to move out and check the other side of the clearing.

The small Cambodian trooper moved forward in a low crouch. Then it happened! They had searched for the enemy until the enemy found them. The early morning stillness was broken by two rapid cracks of a Russian-made AK-47 Kalishnikov assault rifle. The point man jerked upright and then tumbled backwards; his body twitched and then lay still in the position of death. It was no longer quiet as all hell broke loose. Heavy automatic weapons fire cut through the tall grass like a giant scythe.

Without an order from him, Patterson's Cambodians automatically moved into line and began returning fire. Patterson found himself loading a second clip of ammo into the Swedish K before he realized he had fired the first. In a firefight, you do things in the first few seconds without thinking because you have trained to do them. It often determines the outcome of the battle.

The din of the engagement gradually increased into a deafening crescendo. Bullets cracked, screamed and whined, and the strong smell of cordite rose in the air. It is this smell that gets into the warrior's blood and stays there forever; like the smell of death or burning flesh, it is unique. There were cries of wounded and dying men now on both sides of the little clearing. A small Cambodian on Patterson's left grunted and slumped forward. An American sergeant reached down to assist the stricken soldier. A round had taken off the top of his head, and gray matter sprinkled with red oozed out on the ground. Patterson jerked back as if stung by a bee! The strong taste of bile rolled in his stomach and climbed up into his mouth. He felt an instant of guilt because he couldn't remember the dead soldier's name.

Then, in the distance, he heard the familiar hollow thump of mortar rounds leaving the tube. A few seconds later the ground quivered as explosions smashed behind them. The next volley was closer as the Communists began walking the rounds toward his unit. The bulk of the small arms fire was coming from the tree line across the clearing. The Commies had heavy machine guns and mortars so they had to be at least company-size. It was too large a unit for his platoon to tackle. The Commies had him outmanned and outgunned. His weapons were no match for the enemy's. Patterson realized that his unit had stepped into deep problems!

They had to break contact! Patterson shouted over his shoulder to Sergeant Muang, his platoon sergeant. "Break contact! Fall back! Take the dead and wounded!"

There was no way they were going to be able to get the point man. To send someone after his body would be suicide. His men were well drilled in breaking contact and each knew what to do. First, the wounded and dead were dragged to the rear. Then one-half of the platoon laid down a base of fire while the other half "hauled ass" 25 or 30 meters. Then the rear group laid down the fire while the first group pulled back.

However, the Commies were not about to allow the Special Forces Unit to break contact. They'd come for a fight this day, and they'd brought their lunch with them. Each time the Mobile Guerrilla Force fell back, the Communists pushed forward. They were using "hugging tactics."

Off to Patterson's right front, a squad of NVA rose as one and charged! They were cut down as if slapped by a giant hand. The last one performed a little twisting toe dance and hung in the air for an instant before he spun into the damp earth. He won't do that again, thought Patterson.

He had to have some help. It was apparent that his unit wouldn't be able to break contact on their own. To make matters worse, his men were getting short of ammo. A break-contact maneuver uses up a lot of ammo, fast! Patterson beckoned for his radio operator. Ong crawled to his side. He reached over and picked up the mike.

"RAINBOW BASE, THIS IS CHINA BOY EIGHT, OVER."

A voice with a heavy accent, Mexican or Puerto Rican, answered immediately: "CHINA BOY EIGHT, THEES EES RAINBOW BASE. HAVE YOU LIMA CHARLIE (loud and clear). SEND YOUR MESSAGE, OVER."

"RAINBOW, THIS IS CHINA BOY EIGHT. WE ARE IN CONTACT WITH NVA COMPANY, VICINITY CHECK POINT GOLD. NEED GUNSHIPS AND AIR SUPPORT ASAP! NEED AMMO RESUPPLY AND MEDEVAC, SOONEST. OVER."

There was a slight pause, then his radio crackled again: "CHINA BOY EIGHT, THEES EES RAINBOW. MESSAGE UNDERSTOOD. WILL GET BACK TO YOU ASAP, OUT."

The nearest friendly artillery was at Tay Ninh and he was at least five miles from their range. He needed more ammo and gunships if he wanted to get his unit that far. The tactics remained the same for the next half hour: lay down a base of fire, haul ass. Base of fire, haul ass. The Commies kept coming forward; ammo was getting desperate; and still no answer from Rainbow Base!

Finally, they found their backs up against an open rice paddy. When they tried to move right, they ran into heavy fire. They were flanked!

A voice came over his radio: "CHINA BOY EIGHT, THIS IS RAINBOW BASE, OVER." It was a different voice this time, a more authoritative voice.

Patterson flopped down behind the rice paddy dike. He had to catch his voice before he could answer: "THIS IS CHINA BOY EIGHT, OVER."

"THIS IS BASE. AIR SUPPORT HAS BEEN REQUESTED. NONE AVAILABLE NOW BECAUSE OF PRIORITY MISSION. THERE WILL BE A DELAY IN GUNSHIPS AND RESUPPLY. THERE ARE NO BIRDS AT THIS LOCATION TO FLY MISSION! OVER."

Panic rolled up Patterson's back like a gigantic tidal wave—then it subsided to cold fury! He screamed into the microphone: "WHAT THE FUCK—YOU MEAN THERE'S NO HELICOPTERS THERE. WE ARE GETTING THE SHIT SHOT OUT OF US. AT LEAST GET US AMMO!"

The voice of authority returned: "THIS IS BASE. WE ARE DOING EVERYTHING WE CAN. HOW LONG CAN YOU HOLD OUT, OVER."

Patterson was shaking with anger. The fury of battle rose and fell around him. His men were trying to conserve their ammo, putting out a decreasing volume of fire. The enemy, sensing the kill was close, increased their fire and began tightening the ring around his small force. It suddenly dawned on him. He was going to die today! And it had been such a beautiful sunrise.

He shouted into the mike: "HOW THE FUCK SHOULD I KNOW HOW LONG WE CAN HOLD OUT! YOU GOD-DAMNED SONSABITCHES! YOU SHOULD NEVER SEND US OUT HERE WITHOUT A WAY TO SUPPORT US! YOU CAN ALL GO TO HELL!"

He threw the mike down and rolled over into a firing position. By God, he didn't plan on dying easy! There was no way they were going to capture him. He started making mental plans for his next move. He figured their best bet was to scatter in small teams and try to E & E (escape and evade) to Tri-Be or Tay Ninh. He put his weapon down and pulled out his map from the case and began studying it. Then his radio operator began speaking excitedly in Cambodian. He held the mike out to Patterson. The American sergeant took it.

A calm familiar voice came over the airways: "CHINA BOY EIGHT, THIS IS CHINA BOY FIVE, OVER."

Patterson knew that voice well and the call sign was Major Bo Gritz, his commander! But Gritz was supposed to be in Saigon!

Patterson answered: "CHINA BOY FIVE, THIS IS EIGHT. WE GOT BIG TROUBLE DOWN HERE. NVA COMPANY. ALMOST OUT OF AMMO AND THOSE NO GOOD SONSABITCHES AT BASE DON'T HAVE A HELICOPTER TO BRING US ANY!"

Gritz spoke back calmly: "HEY BROTHER! CALM DOWN! STACK MAGAZINES AND THROW GRENADES. I'LL BE THERE IN FIFTEEN MINUTES, WITH AMMO!"

Sometimes words can perform miracles, and Bo's words did just that! A flood of relief poured through Patterson. Somehow, he knew that Gritz would be there in a few minutes with ammo and everything would be all right. Bo's words were always law! His promises were always kept. He felt as if he was a drowning man who had just been tossed a life preserver. He calmly passed his next order to his platoon sergeant: "Hold positions and conserve ammo. Major Bo's coming!"

Gritz had been flying from Saigon back to the SFOB (Special Forces Operating Base) at Tay Ninh, when he monitored Patterson's call for help. After reassuring his desperate platoon leader, he flew on into Tay Ninh and filled his chopper with ammo. Fifteen minutes later he was circling over the beleagured platoon.

Patterson looked up and saw the chopper. He figured that Bo would hover behind them and kick out the ammo. Gritz called him: "CHINA BOY EIGHT. POP SMOKE, OVER."

Patterson pulled the pin and tossed a yellow smoke grenade into the rice paddy and then spoke into his mike: "CHINA BOY FIVE, THIS IS EIGHT, SMOKE OUT, OVER."

"I IDENTIFY YELLOW SMOKE, OVER."

"THAT'S CORRECT. YELLOW SMOKE."

The helicopter settled into the paddy almost vertically. The pilot stopped at a hover about four feet from the ground. Patterson's men were laying down a heavy base of fire to try to keep the enemy gunners from zeroing in on the chopper. Gritz kicked the boxes out. Then he jumped into the mud. Cambodes ran out to retrieve the ammo. The helicopter pilot pulled pitch and roared back up into the air. Bo ran in a zig-zag pattern to Patterson's side.

With a fresh supply of ammo, and Patterson's morale boosted by Gritz's presence, the platoon began fighting a withdrawal action. Thirty minutes later, they were within friendly artillery range. When the high explosive 155's began crashing into the enemy's rank, the battle turned and the NVA broke contact and pulled out. Patterson's casualties were 4 KIA and 10 WIA. It could have been worse; and it would have, if it hadn't been for Bo Gritz. There was no doubt that he saved their lives that day. The ammo resupply alone might have made the difference, but most commanders would not have joined the unit on the ground. Bo Gritz did!

A former second lieutenant in the South Vietnamese Army reports that he was imprisoned, through 1975, at a camp Tan Canh. He said that a group of Americans led by a Major, were kept in a separate compound more than a kilometer from the South Vietnamese. He had opportunities to communicate with the Americans, and did so in English; the major had served in the Cavalry Brigade assigned to the defense of Dac To and Tan Canh and had been captured in 1971. There were also two American sergeants and a first lieutenant there. The major was short, thin, and had a long face, a bald forehead, brown eyes and long eyebrows. His nose is a little flattened between the eyes, a dimple in the middle of his chin, teeth distant from another. The Vietnamese prisoner used to be ordered to bring sweet potatoes to the 'American pirates;' they had their hands and legs tied up when they weren't working. The Americans were building roads.

BOEITCHER, THOMAS B.
"We Can Keep You Forever"
National Review Magazine,
August 1981

CHAPTER THIRTEEN

LAOS, 28 NOVEMBER 1982

The first bivouac was established about four miles west of Highway 13. Three Lao, with the UZI's, were placed out on security while the remainder of the patrol rested and ate. Zappone, the Team medic, checked the feet of the Americans: Gritz's were already like hamburger and "Zap" burst some of the blisters and applied antiseptic and tough skin. Patterson's were white and water logged, but so far no blisters. He put on fresh socks and a lot of foot powder. Goldman and Zappone had a few blisters, but nothing serious. The rice paddies were dry and one would think this would make for easier walking, and that was true to an extent. Actually, they could move faster, but the cement-hard rough texture was difficult to walk on and tough on the feet.

They were carrying LRRP rations which were first used during the Vietnam war by special units. The regular combat units still carried the old "C-rations" which were nothing more than canned food. The C-rations were heavy and bulky to carry. LRRP (pronounced 'lurp') rations are packets of dehydrated food, which require the addition of boiling water. The same type of rations can be purchased over-the-counter now for hiking, fishing, hunting, etc., and they are usually quite expensive. One problem with LRRPs is that when you are on a clandestine operation behind the enemy lines, you cannot or should not build fires. So, you are unable to have boiling water. The GI's solution to this problem was to add tepid water from their canteen to the packet, then continue to carry it for several hours. The result is a little crunchy and not nearly as delicious as when the food is "grabbed" by boiling water —but it helps to fill you up and the taste depends upon the degree of hunger.

All through the day they could hear convoys rumble by on Highway 13, and there were occasional sounds of artillery fire to the south. Around noon, a small single engine airplane flew low over their position. They all scrambled over next to the stream and watched the plane carefully for signs of any spray. According to the Lao, if you immerse yourself in water, it will protect you from the "yellow rain." It didn't rain yellow that day, and the plane flew on south. A little later, a two-engine plane flew over, going north. The Lao said it was the daily courier flight from Vinh Tinh to Savannakhet and back to Vinh Tinh. The remainder of the day passed quietly and they moved out that evening at 2100 hours.

It was the period of the full moon. There was no need to wear the night vision goggles in the moonlight—it was bright enough to read a book. It was a comfortable night and everyone's spirits were high. At first, they moved cautiously because they were near Highway 13, and according to intelligence reports, the road was patrolled by a Communist battalion. The point man signaled and they stopped short of the road. Two Lao went across and checked the other side. Then they moved up to the road, got on line and everyone rushed across the road at one time. Highway 13 was in surprisingly good condition, a super highway by Asian standards. It was so light, you could see a mile in each direction.

A few clouds appeared, so once across the highway, they put on the night vision goggles and moved rapidly for two more hours.

29 NOVEMBER 1982

At 0400 hours, Gritz called a halt. They were exhausted! The heavy packs combined with the deteriorating condition of their feet forced them to stop sooner than they wanted. The infantryman's primary mode of transportation is his feet. A tanker has to maintain his tank to fight. When his tank breaks down, the tank is no longer an effective fighting machine. When an infantryman's feet break down, he is no longer an effective fighting machine, so he must care for his feet with the same dedication.

The patrol moved into a dense woodline and set up security. Patterson popped the release on his rucksack and let it slide to the ground. He felt as if he had been carrying the weight of the world on his back, and he wondered if he would ever be able to straighten up again! He was too tired to set up his hammock so he just wrapped up in his poncho liner and fell into a deep, exhausted sleep. It is when a soldier becomes this worn out that he is the most lax and most vulnerable. He gets to the point where he just doesn't care. That is why good physical condition is so important to the soldier. A man in good shape will get tired—but he recovers quickly.

Around 0600 hours, something awakened Patterson. He sat up to see four or five Lao standing around a large fire, chattering. The dense black smoke curled up above the trees. They seemed unconcerned that they were deep in enemy territory! He threw aside his poncho liner, jumped up, walked over to the Lao, and kicked the closest one square on the ass! "Put that damned fire out!" he ordered, in Thai.

The commotion woke up Bo, who joined Patterson. Together they kicked dirt on the fire. The Lao knew that they had done wrong. They sheepishly scattered and went back to their bedrolls.

Zappone made another foot check. They all had blisters that needed attention. Gritz's socks were coated with blood and had to be peeled off his feet. He had to be hurting! But he didn't complain. The Lao had a mixture of foot gear: tennis shoes, sandals, jungle boots and street shoes. But they were used to trekking through the jungle and had formed hard callouses on their feet. They could have done just as well barefooted, but footwear of any kind was a luxury to them. Take away their uniforms and weapons and you would see stone age people in breechcloths. It seemed only that the accoutrements of war had given them a modern tinge.

Bo walked over and sat down beside Patterson. "How're you holding up, Pat?"

"Hell! I'm doing fine. How're your feet?"

"They're a mite sore, but I'll get by."

"I'm gonna kill that fuckin' Wilson for not sending the hand-cranked generator!" declared Patterson, not really meaning the threat.

"I'm beginning to wonder which side that son-of-a-bitch is on!" said Gritz, matter-of-factly.

"I'll be glad when we link up with Kham Bou tomorrow. I feel naked without a weapon. I hope he makes it to the rendezvous."

"I think he will. I trust these guys. So far, there's been no problem," returned Gritz. "How do you think Zap is doing?"

"He impresses me as a damned good soldier! I just wish he had some combat experience behind him. Maybe I ought to sneak out ahead and give him the Mexican Knife trick."

Gritz laughed. "You still haven't forgiven me for the Mexican Knife, have you?"

"Hell no! You almost blew my head off!" Patterson grumbled, smiling.

They were talking about an incident that occurred in Vietnam in 1968. There was a Colonel named Ryan who worked on the B-Team staff. Ryan was really too old for combat and everybody accused him of being George Washington's supply officer. Ryan's code name was "Mexican Knife." Everyone liked the Colonel and considered him a gentleman of the old school.

One day, Bo approached Patterson. "Colonel Ryan is going home soon and I want to give him this captured CHICOM (Chinese Communist) carbine. Now, Ryan has been shot at a few times but he has never had a chance to shoot at anybody since he's been here. So we're going to make a big hero out of him and give him one good war story to talk about when he gets home."

Patterson looked questioningly at his boss, not quite sure that he wanted to hear the answer to his question: "Oh! How are we going to do that?"

"I want you to go to the old Soui Da Camp. Take this CHICOM carbine with you. Get a bag of chicken blood and some captured Ho Chi Minh sandals. Take a couple of Cambodes with you so they can cover your back. Just lay up out there across from the old airstrip and when you see us drive up, you open fire on us. We'll return a little fire, and you break the bag of blood and leave the carbine and sandals, then di di (Vietnamese for run)."

Patterson figured that sounded like a good idea. He liked Colonel Ryan. "Okay! That's the least we can do for Mexican Knife."

Two hours later, Patterson was in position. He didn't know what pretext Gritz was going to use to get Ryan to come with him, but he knew they would show. Sure enough, here came Bo and Colonel Ryan. The jeep stopped on the old airstrip and the two men dismounted and started talking. Patterson put the carbine up to his shoulder and squeezed off several rounds that kicked up the dust near the American officers.

Of course, no one told the Colonel that this was just a joke and he was evidently a better shot than anyone suspected. Gritz and the Colonel both jumped behind the jeep and returned fire. Suddenly things were hot and heavy around Patterson as the bullets whined past his head and kicked up dust in his face. He suddenly wondered how Gritz would explain the death of one of his own sergeants. Patterson popped the bag of blood and began to wriggle in one of the lowest crawls of his career—six inches below the ground —to the rear. Bullets were blazing all around him like a swarm of angry bees. He finally made it into the jungle where he took off!

When Gritz and Colonel Ryan returned to the main camp, the Colonel was grinning from ear to ear. He had captured a CHICOM carbine which he could take home with him—and had probably killed himself a Communist. From the amount of blood loss, he couldn't have lived long!

A smiling Gritz looked at Patterson and winked. Patterson gave his superior officer "the finger."

A little later, Patterson sidled up to Gritz and whispered, "Hey boss, those bullets were coming awfully gawd-damned close to me!"

Bo just laughed. "We had to make it look real!"

Colonel Ryan left Vietnam three days later with his CHICOM carbine and one damned good war story.

Gritz woke Patterson out of his daydream, "No, Pat, I won't ask you to do the Mexican Knife trick this trip!"

Countless hours of testimony have been taken from refugees claiming to have seen American captives. As of May 10, 1980, The Defense Intelligence Agency was checking out 370 "live sighting" reports alleged to have been made since 1975. Of these, 222 were said to have been firsthand sightings and the remaining heresay. Exhaustive interrogation sessions, including polygraph tests, have convinced even skeptical U.S. authorities that many of the refugee reports are valid.

SINGLAUB, JOHN K.
Major General
U.S. Army, Retired
The American Legion Magazine, 1980

CHAPTER FOURTEEN

They moved out shortly after dark. The movement was slow because of the heavy packs and the deteriorating physical condition of the Americans. The Laos were patient with their farang comrades. Their packs were not nearly as heavy and they were accustomed to jungle walking. The rest stops became more frequent—and longer. At midnight, they rested for two hours; then they pushed on until daylight.

30 NOVEMBER 1982

The patrol holed-up in a small bamboo thicket. They were miles behind schedule and this was the day they were supposed to meet General Kham Bou and his men at the first staging area, near Nhong Khet Laung. Gritz called a strategy meeting. It was decided they had no recourse but to push on in the daylight to reach the rendezvous in time. Once they linked up with Kham Bou and his 100 armed men, they could rest and regroup in relative security before they continued the mission.

A Lao, Nhung Tum, one of Kham Bou's men, knew the area and the location of the rendezvous and took over as point man. Under their heavy loads, which fortunately would be lightened when they reached the first staging area, the Americans plodded on with aching backs and bleeding feet. The area they were moving through was interspersed with small clearings, low ridge lines and thick jungle. They hadn't moved far when the point man suddenly stopped and held up his hand. Every man froze in his tracks. Patterson moved quietly forward and joined the point. There he found a hi-speed trail running east and west. It was covered with fresh bata boot and sandal tracks. A large contingent of troops had passed this way recently, probably within the last two hours.

He moved back and explained the situation to Gritz. The patrol pulled back into the jungle and set up listening posts. They watched and waited for one hour. There was no activity so they crossed the trail and moved slightly south into the thick jungle. The movement here was slower and more difficult, but there was more cover and concealment. Never sacrifice security for speed and comfort, particularly behind enemy lines.

At 1100, they stopped in a small clearing. They were scheduled to make their first radio contact with Lance Trimmer in Nakhon Phanom at 1400 hours. The tall trees surrounding the clearing were ideal to string up their jungle antennae. They tried unsuccessfully for 30 minutes to reach their base station.

"We'll just have to move to higher ground," said Gritz.

The equipment was repacked and the patrol moved on for two more hours. Finally, they located what looked like an ideal spot on a ridge line which should give them a straight shot back to Thailand. They were located just west of Phou Hin Ang mountain, and a few miles south of Ban Nong Khet Laung. Gary Goldman and Dominic Zappone sat down, released their rucks and began removing the radio and equipment. Patterson sat down, and as he learned to do in Vietnam, he instinctively put his back up against a tree. Gritz was on his right, Goldman was on Bo's right, and next to him was Zappone. Patterson heaved a big sigh of relief and reached up and popped the release on his rucksack. He looked up to see Nhung Tum, the point man who was carrying his UZI, turn around with a look of fear on his face. He said only one word, in English: "Communists!"

With an ear shattering crack, the bark peeled off the tree next to Patterson's head as an AK-47 opened up on full automatic! If he hadn't had his back against the tree, the burst of fire would have taken his head off! He didn't have his ruck on, and his first instinct was *fuck that rucksack!*

He rolled back to the left and peeled into the jungle. Gritz was right behind him, with his ruck still on, followed by Gary Goldman and a scrambling bunch of Lao. No sooner had they hit the jungle than 60mm mortar rounds began crashing ahead of them, blocking their route of escape. With Patterson leading, the group veered to the south and ran "hell for leather" for 200 meters. Patterson pulled up in a bamboo thicket and began taking head count as his comrades joined him: "Nine, ten, eleven, twelve Lao!" He didn't have to count to see that there were only two Americans, besides himself. They were missing three Lao and one American. He looked around. "Where the hell is Zap?" He turned to Gritz. "Zap's missing!"

Gritz looked around the group. "Where'd he go? What happened? I thought we were all together!"

Patterson shook his head. He tried to catch his breath. "Three Lao are gone, too—and two were carrying the UZI's. Shit!" He turned to the nearest Lao and spoke in Thai: "Where is the other American?"

The Lao whom they called the Fat Man spoke up: "He run the other way—to the enemy!"

Patterson translated for Gritz and Goldman; then he turned to the Montagnard Chief, Akhein, who was carrying the third UZI and was up near the point man when the firing started: "What happened back there? Did you see?"

Akhein answered, "Communists! Three Lao die, one American chop (they caught him)!"

"Are you sure?"

"Yes, I sure."

"How do you know?"

"I see!"

Patterson translated for the Americans. They took stock of their situation. They had one UZI and one pistol. The Americans had one rucksack with six rations. The Lao still had their rucks, but they were filled with medical supplies. Zappone was missing! They had no idea whether he was dead, captured or lost. Three Laotians were missing. One of them, the point man, was the only man on the whole patrol who knew where the rendezvous with Kham Bou would be!

"Ask Akhein if he will go back and look for the Lao and the American," said Gritz.

Patterson passed on the request, and Akhein agreed to comply. The little Montagnard moved out quickly. A few minutes later Patterson heard yelling in the distance. He thought he heard two different voices but he couldn't be positive. They waited for a tense 45 minutes before Akhein returned. Patterson greeted him with "Who were you yelling at?"

"I try to find American and three Lao."

"Did you find anything?"

"No! I see Communists where they go back down ravine."

"Were the packs gone?"

"Yes. Packs all gone!"

"Are you sure they were Communists and not Free Lao?"

"Yes!"

"How do you know?"

"I see!"

Patterson passed on to Gritz what the chief had said.

"Ask him if he thinks we should go on," directed Gritz.

Patterson knew that was a stupid question. One look at Akhein, the Fat Man and the other Lao would give you the answer. Obviously, they were all scared! The ambush had taken away their resolve. Of course, the fact they didn't have any weapons probably didn't help matters. He turned to the Laos. "Do you think we should go on?"

Akhein answered for the others. "No! We should go back to Thailand. Too many Communists in area. Now they know Americans are here, many more will come quick. We must go!"

Patterson translated, then added, "It's 65 to 70 miles back. I think we've come too far to go back now. Besides, we can't leave Zappone!"

They were all worried about Zappone. When the shooting started, everyone stuck together except Zap. That's where combat experience pays off. Zap didn't pull with the rest of the Special Forces vets—in fact, he went the opposite direction. The other Americans didn't notice because they were too busy getting themselves out of the immediate area. Patterson realized that things like this—what to do if they were ambushed; what if they ran into enemy forces but no shots were fired; what if someone was injured or wounded—should have been discussed before they left Thailand, perhaps even have been rehearsed. But they were not. It was simply damned poor planning. With combat seasoned troops, it would have been automatic—everybody sticks together and you "shag ass." Even experienced soldiers need to rehearse. If Zap is dead, thought Patterson, it will be on my conscience for the rest of my life.

"With our guide gone, we'll never be able to rendezvous with Kham Bou," said a very disgusted Goldman. He had wanted to be part of a successful rescue mission more than anything else in his life.

Gritz laid it out for them: "We don't know where to look for Zap, and we can't do any good without weapons. We could go on to the next staging area, but without weapons and food it would be too risky. The Lao don't want to go on, so they won't be worth a damn to us! I hate like hell to scrub the mission and go back, especially without Zap, but I don't see any other recourse. We have to go back!"

Patterson's first inclination was to protest, but on second thought, he realized that Bo and Gary were right. It was like Bo to make the decision without getting others' opinions, but that was his way, and Patterson knew it was the correct way.

Gritz continued, "We'll go back. We'll get the weapons from the Thais, even if we have to take them by force, and then we'll come back, locate Zap and go on with the mission!"

They took off at a half-run, with Akhein leading. They ran for three hours, then they rested for 15 minutes and resumed their flight. They avoided the approach route by circling well to the south.

About midnight, they came to a deep ravine with a log across it. Akhein scurried across, then it became Patterson's turn. He almost made it! There was a crack as the log broke and suddenly he was falling. His side bounced hard against the log and he felt a numbing pain in his rib cage. Then he was in the air and tumbling. The rocks in the bottom of the ravine broke his fall. The log came down on his foot. There was a piercing pain as a slice of the log drove through the top of his left foot. He lay there, trying to catch his breath. Each breath brought intense pain to his ribs. He tried to stand up, but he could not. His foot was stuck to a limb. He looked down to see a sliver of wood protruding from the top of his jungle boot! Goldman and Gritz scrambled down the steep embankment and joined him.

"Are you okay?" asked a worried Gritz.

"It's my foot! I ran a stick through it!"

Gritz knelt beside him and examined the foot with his flashlight. Patterson had visions of becoming incapacitated. He understood the difficulty the two Americans and the small Lao would have in trying to carry him 50 miles to the Thai border. Goldman grasped his leg and Gritz jerked the stick from his foot. It hurt a lot more coming out than it did going in. The thing had gone clear through his foot!

1 DECEMBER 1982

They moved on until just before daylight. Every step caused excruciating pain for Patterson. Only the adrenaline of the fear of being left behind, or captured, kept him going. His ribs hurt like hell and he was beginning to think a couple were broken. When they stopped, he eased himself to the ground and gingerly removed his boot. The foot was throbbing and starting to swell. He tried to sleep but he couldn't get comfortable. His injuries were on opposite sides: left foot, right side of chest. To get any relief, he had to put pressure on one or the other and it wasn't working. Nobody tended him. Everyone was in that state of exhaustion where they had all they could do to keep themselves going. Finally, he either passed out or slipped into a troubled sleep, and he slipped back in time. He was back in Vietnam.

It was Christmas Eve 1967—or was it '68? It really didn't make much difference—but it was Christmas Eve, a time to be home, a time to celebrate with family and friends and to give thanks for peace on earth, good will to men! He was sitting in the Tri-Be Special Forces Club, celebrating in his own way; and he was half to three-quarters drunk, trying to forget what day it was and where he was.

His team captain walked up with a sergeant in tow. "Pat, this is Sergeant Larry Putnam; he just arrived today. This is his first tour in Nam. I want you to take him out with you tomorrow and break his cherry."

Patterson was scheduled to take out a 200-man, company-sized, mixed Vietnamese and Cambode patrol on Christmas Day, for a five-day Search and Destroy mission. He looked up at the new sergeant through booze-clouded eyes and said, sarcastically: "Oh! A cherry boy. Well, we'll take care of that. By tomorrow noon I'll either have you in one hell-of-a-fight, or we'll both be dead!" He didn't really believe what he was saying but the booze was talking with bravado. Besides, it was something his idol Bo Gritz would say!

They moved out of the compound at 0500 the next morning. An early morning walk in the jungle is one sure way to sober up. At 0900, the column halted and Patterson went forward to see what was up. He found enemy communications wire strung above the trail between two trees. Patterson cut the wire and tied off one end; then he set his men up in a horseshoe-shaped ambush.

Twenty minutes later a force of "Charlies" came jogging down the trail to repair their broken commo line. Patterson allowed them to get into the killing zone of the claymores, then he pushed the detonator. (Claymores are directional mines, which, when exploded, send thousands of small steel fragments in an expanding Vee toward the enemy.) The morning quiet was shattered! The first group of Viet Cong were blasted off their feet like tenpins! Five were killed instantly. Their shattered bodies looked like someone had torn apart a bunch of rag dolls and haphazardly thrown their parts up and down the trail! The trailing VC took cover and opened up in a desperate attempt to escape the ambush.

Sergeant Putnam, who was kneeling behind a tree squeezing off short bursts, looked over at Patterson. "Damn! You weren't bullshitting me, were you?"

Patterson smiled back and shrugged his shoulders. "Welcome to Vietnam."

A successful ambush is one that is set up so that once the enemy walks into the killing zone and the ambush is triggered, every man in the zone is killed. This was a perfect ambush. The Fort Benning Ranger School would have been proud! When the firefight was over, not one friendly was injured. Twelve VC died for Uncle Ho!

Patterson called in a situation report. A helicopter dropped in and resupplied them and the company pushed on.

They spent the next two days with no enemy contact. Several rice caches were located and destroyed. At 2000 hours the third night, the column was moving cautiously along a heavily used jungle trail. The point-man stopped and raised his weapon, signaling: "Enemy in sight!"

Patterson inched his way to the front of the column with Putnam following. Some 100 meters ahead of them was the light of a campfire, flickering through the trees. Patterson leaned over and whispered to his fellow sergeant, "I'm going to take a look-see." He motioned for the point-man to follow him. They got down on their bellies and slithered off the trail into the jungle.

Shortly after they started, Patterson heard a noise to his right. It couldn't be the point-man because he was right behind him. He stopped. The noise quit! He moved out again, inching toward the clearing ahead. There was the noise again! He stopped. The noise stopped! He was now about 40 meters from the clearing. He raised his head. There were a bunch of VC cooking their evening meal. A strong smell of Nuc Mam (a very potent-smelling fish sauce that the Viets put on just about everything) filled the air. He heard the noise on his right again and then a metallic click. He looked over to see an equally surprised VC four feet from him. They evidently had been crawling together on a parallel course. The VC was faster. He fired first—two quick shots! Patterson's face and head exploded in a kaleidoscope of pain! He instinctively squeezed the trigger on the Swedish K and fired the entire magazine of 36 rounds. Then he slumped face forward in a widening pool of blood.

The VC camp became a blur of activity as they scattered in all directions. Some of them went the wrong way and were cut down by his force. The little Cambode point-man took one look at his leader and ran back to the column. He solemnly announced to Putnam, "Sergeant Pat dead!"

Putnam grabbed the Cambode and pushed him back up the trail. "Show me!"

Patterson, hit in the head and face, had not lost consciousness; however, his motor senses were not working. He couldn't move!

Putnam leaned over him and whispered, "How bad you hit?"

Patterson wanted to say, "I'm dying, you dumb shit! Do something!" He tried to talk, but with nine teeth shot away all he could do was mumble as the blood filled his mouth.

Putnam rolled Patterson up on his side. It was a good move; it probably saved him from choking to death on his own blood. Then he draped his poncho so it would shield the light. He took out his lighter and flicked it on so he could examine his fallen comrade.

Patterson heard a "HOLY SHIT!" Thinking Putnam was referring to his condition, Patterson went into shock and passed into black unconsciousness!

He didn't find out—until four months later, when he returned to his unit and talked to the then highly decorated combat veteran who saved his life, Sergeant Larry Putnam—that Putnam's exclamation was brought about by his seeing the Commie that Patterson had shot. The 36 rounds blasted the VC's head clean off!

My friend was on a bus enroute to Saigon in September 1979 when it was attacked by a squad of eight "resistance soldiers." The squad boarded the bus; three of the eight were Americans. The Americans requested that any of the passengers with access to the outside world transmit news of their situation to American authorities, saying that originally there had been five Americans in the group but two had died. They also recited their names but my friend could not remember them.

BOETTCHER, THOMAS D. and
REHYANSKI, JOSEPH A.
"We Can Keep you Forever"
National Review, 1981

CHAPTER FIFTEEN

LAOS, 1 DECEMBER 1982

Patterson's mind tried to shed the dark veil and transcend into the conscious world. He was shot in the head! Again? The hole he was trying to climb out of was deep, dark, and smelled of death. He awoke with a start! Where was he? Vietnam? No, that was a long time ago. He was having a dream, but a dream that had really happened. He sat up, shivering; his torn fatigues were drenched with sweat. Patterson looked down at his foot. It was swollen to twice its normal size! He removed his sock and found small red streaks climbing his ankle. Infection! He had blood poisoning! He should never have removed his boot because he wouldn't be able to get it back on. His head was hot. He had a fever. How in hell would he ever make it back to Thailand? He didn't want to be left behind, abandoned like Zap!

Patterson rested fitfully the rest of the day. When it came time to move out, he and Gritz struggled and finally succeeded in getting his boot over his swollen foot. But they had to split the side and the toe. The first half hour was agonizing, and then the foot numbed to the movement. It became a matter of just placing one foot in front of the other and leaning forward. There is an old infantryman's axiom: "When the time comes and your strength is gone and the body pleads to quit, and you are positive you can't go any further, your guts must take over and order your mind to move. Left foot forward! Swing right foot past left foot! Don't think! Don't feel! Just swing the feet and move. Swing and move!"

All three Americans were in poor shape: dehydrated; weak from lack of nourishment; and feet cut, torn and bleeding. Goldman, the marathoner, was holding up best. He was scheduled to swim the river and bring back the boats to pick up his comrades.

The Fat Man, walking point, suddenly walked the patrol right into a well-populated village, full of uniformed soldiers—North Vietnamese and Pathet Lao! The rescue team did an about face and beat a hasty retreat; however, not before the dogs spotted them. The raiders moved as fast as they could, which wasn't nearly as fast as they would have wished. Voices joined the barking dogs and stayed behind them. Finally, after two hours, the sound of pursuit faded away.

They were forced to quit at midnight. They were too exhausted to go any further without rest. Gritz had wanted to reach the river on 1 December, but now that was impossible.

2 DECEMBER 1982

The team moved out early the next morning. Patterson's foot seemed a little better. After two hours, exhaustion hit them again. Since they missed the opportunity for Goldman to swim the river on the 1st, it was decided that all three Americans, along with Akhein and Boun Thong, would swim across the night of the 2nd. The remainder of the patrol would stay in Laos with most of the equipment. Once in Thailand, Gritz and his party would regroup, rest, re-equip, and return on 4 December. This was rather an ambitious plan considering the physical condition of the Americans and the fact that no arrangements had been made to pick up arms and equipment.

Sometime during the rest stop, the Fat Man took off with Bo's pistol. He was carrying it because he had been walking point.

At 1400 hours, Gritz, Goldman, Patterson and Akhein moved out. Akhein was leading and packing the only weapon left, the

UZI. Two other Lao were accompanying them as far as the river. They were going to bring back any equipment the team didn't take across the river.

At 1500 hours, they ran into the Fat Man. His village was near so he simply took a short AWOL to scrounge some food. He was carrying a banana leaf piled high with sticky rice and fish, which they all shared. He informed them that the villagers said that because of the holiday the Vietnamese and Pathet Lao patrols would all be in by 1700 hours.

They rested and resumed their march at 1600 hours. Ahead lay the mile-wide Mekong, and beyond that, safety. Patterson's obviously infected foot throbbed, but he felt he could make the last 15 miles. Whether or not he could make the swim once he got there was another question.

The final dash to the Mekong was difficult and exhausting. Several days later, Gary Goldman wrote about that last night:

Approximately 1800 hours, we began moving again, and this time continued for the remainder of the cross-country phase. We were able to keep the Fat Man (Boun Thong) and Akhein headed on a generally westerly direction. But once again we zigged and zagged constantly. We were moving at an approximate rate of 4 to 5 kilometers per hour and it was steady. We headed down a major trail with white sand for a fairly long period, then we hit the rice paddy area. We would stop approximately every 70 minutes for a rest and we replenished our water supply on occasion. Movement wasn't actually difficult. It was just that our feet had been so badly battered the past few days that taking each step was an excruciating experience in pain. We were all clumsy and waddled like penguins. The paddies were mostly dry, which means very rough. The combination of the rough surface and the dikes with our by now lousy sense of balance was exhausting. We were wringing wet with sweat, even though it was a relatively clear and mild might. The moon rose at approximately 1930, and the sky had a high cover of cirrostratus. The rapid and constant march, combined with the empty Laotian countryside bathed by the full moon beaming through the clouds, gave the night a very strangely beautiful and hypnotic quality. It was surreal, bizarre, and yet I was having a hell of a good time. I'm not sure if it wasn't the combination of exhaustion, pain, or what—but I seemed exhilarated. It was strange. When we stopped, I would look up at the sky and watch the clouds move steadily like some gossamer curtain past the face of the moon and could only break away by force of will. The first few moments of movement after these little episodes were very disorienting—you had to concentrate on walking to snap out of it.

We moved at a fairly constant rate, skirting villages, crossing paddies, hearing voices and barking dogs on occasion. We had long since run out of halazone, and I know that we drank some 'non-FDA' approved water, a lot of dirt, shit, piss and corruption. It was a constant battle to keep the Laos on an azimuth. They either don't believe it, or they just can't resist a trail that heads somewhere within 180 degrees of where you want to go. One of the younger Laos with whom I spent some time explaining the intricacies of LRRP rations, began to pass pieces of a slightly sweet, oniony root to us. It was crunchy, delicious and seemed to give us a bit of added strength. He seemed genuinely concerned about us and kept pushing, cajoling, and generally kept us moving. Finally, approximately 2130, he pointed out the red lights on the radio tower of That Phanom. After a few more zigs and zags, which were all the more frustrating since we could practically see where we were going, we finally reached the Mekong. Unfortunately, we were at a point where there were nearby islands, well south of That Phanom. We marched north, parallelling the river for approximately one km. The Laos began to make preparations for the crossing. They cut down banana trees to float on, and when I looked at Akhein, he was stark naked with his clothes wrapped in a sarong strapped in a bundle around his waist. One hand covered his genitals, the other held a big piece of log over his right shoulder. Two days out of the stone age, with a pair of night vision goggles around his neck, there in the Laotian moonlight, what a picture! We finally made it to the crossing point—a sandy beach four miles south of That Phanom."

The Lao were busily hacking away at banana trees. At first Patterson was puzzled; then he realized they were making logs upon which they could float across the Mekong. The Americans, by now almost totally exhausted, elected to rig their canteens as floats, and swim across. They didn't think they would be able to stay on the rolling logs. There was no conversation now; everyone knew what they wanted to do—swim the river which couldn't be swum! The Americans stripped to their shorts and walked into the Mekong at 2300 hours. A few yards out, the current grabbed them and Goldman and Akhein disappeared. Gritz was near Patterson for awhile and then he, too, was gone. The cool water felt good to Patterson's throbbing foot. He kept stroking, fighting against the vicious current that was sweeping him downstream. After one hour he looked back. It seemed as if he had only gone a couple hundred meters. Up ahead he spotted what he thought was a boat; it swept past him heading north, up the river. Another went by, only this time it was closer. It wasn't a boat; it was a damn benchmark in the middle of the river, and it was stationary. He hadn't realized how fast he was going downstream.

Patterson was steadily growing weaker, waves of dizziness floated across his eyes. Stamina is like blood; you only have so much, and when it's gone, your mechanism stops. He continued to stroke, stroke and stroke! Finally, up ahead he saw it—the Thai side of the river. He had made it! Relief flooded through him in gigantic waves. By damn! He'd made it! It took another 30 minutes to reach land. Leaning against the shore, he glanced at his waterproof Seiko. It was 0200 hours. He had been swimming for three hours!

3 DECEMBER 1982

The sergeant pulled himself ashore and lay there, catching his breath. Then he stood up and started walking across the beach. He was on an island. Dejectedly, he sat down on the far side and looked across the stretch of river still remaining. Pieces of wood and flotsam floated past at a dizzying rate. The current ahead appeared to be faster than that behind—probably because he was at a bend of the river. There was no one else in sight. He didn't have any idea whether his comrades were alive or dead. He sat there looking at the other side, saying to himself, "I can make it! I can make it!" After about thirty minutes, he stood up, mumbled to himself, "What the fuck!", and stepped off into the river. He figured there would be a few feet of shallow water, but there wasn't! He stepped in over his head and the current latched onto him, turning him around, and tumbling him over and over. Finally, with a great deal of effort, he got himself straightened out and began swimming, harder than he had at anytime in his life! It seemed as if he wasn't making any headway across—just sailing downstream at an ever increasing rate. He struggled this way for another hour, his strength waning. Then finally his reserve was gone. He'd had the course. He wanted to close his eyes and sleep, just slip below the surface and let the river take him. He thought about his son, Jimmy. He thought about his wife and family— wondered how they'd take the news of his death. Would he become just another of the "missing" in Southeast Asia? Did Virginia really understand how much he loved her? He couldn't raise his arm for one more stroke. Shit! He would rather have cashed in during a good firefight! The fear of what was about to happen to him clouded his mind. Red flashes danced before his eyes and he passed into the world of the unconscious.

He woke up! The current had slowed down; his hand was clutching something sticky—finally, he realized what it was—it was oozing, stinking, wonderful mud. He dragged himself forward, rolled over on his back and laid his head on the bank. Directly above, the stars were laughing down at him. He thought that human beings must seem awfully petty and insignificant compared to a star. Then his mind turned to something really important—a cigarette about six inches thick and four feet long!

A crashing in the bushes above him jarred him out of his lethargy. It sounded like a herd of elephants. If it was a Thai army patrol, they would just have to catch him. He was too tired to move. In fact, he just might not move for a week! In a few minutes, Akhein came stumbling down the bank and joined him. They rested for another 30 minutes, then discussed how hungry they were. Akhein said he had a friend nearby. "We can get food there!"

They climbed the steep bank and came to a dirt road paralleling the Mekong. Akhein informed Patterson that they were seven miles downstream from where they'd entered the water on the other side. The American had swum one mile west and seven miles south, and probably much further when you consider that he was fighting the current. They turned into a pathway and were greeted by barking dogs. The house was typical of the area, built 15 feet above the ground on poles—a sensible way to live during the rainy season. They were soon stuffing themselves with rice balls, kowpot, maklie, and wonderfully hot coffee.

2 DECEMBER 1982, 2300 HOURS

Gary Goldman started off with the breast stroke, then began alternating with the side stroke. Boun Thong was near him, straddling his banana log, frog-kicking and paddling with his hands. The current was stronger than Goldman had imagined. He estimated this trip across the Mekong would take 40 to 50 minutes but he had already been in the water for 50 minutes and the far bank didn't seem any closer. Patterson and Gritz had disappeared long ago. The ex-captain didn't know whether they had been swept downstream, got a cramp and drowned, or were just sucked under by the strong current.

Goldman was close enough to see that every once in awhile Boun Thong would start praying. He wondered if the Lao was praying for himself, or the American, or both? He began to feel the first tinges of a leg cramp. He tried to will it away! He must, because a cramp would be fatal. It was a beautiful night. He recalled Gritz's statement just before the first Mekong crossing. It would be a good night to die—but Gary Goldman decided not to! Forty-five minutes later, his feet touched land. He had made it! And he still felt strong. A piece of cake, he told himself! He had actually enjoyed the swimming—the water felt good massaging his battered feet. He stood up and headed across the beach. Boun Thong followed with the big log over his shoulder. Goldman couldn't understand why the little Lao didn't just drop his log. There was a little water ahead. Goldman slipped on his boots because he figured there would be some pebbles in the shallows ahead. Boun Thong laid his log in the water and climbed on. Goldman stepped into fifteen feet of water and the current swept him away. The beach was only an island, and now he was in the main channel. It was another hour of heavy swimming before he dragged himself ashore in Thailand.

AUTHOR'S NOTE: After all that had happened—two operations cancelled, off and on again government support, personnel problems, financial problems, months of planning and preparation, and three years of waiting—the actual conduct of the raid was incompetent and amateurish.

Any young private, just out of basic training, can tell you that "no one would invade enemy territory with 19 men armed with three semi-automatic weapons." You can "sneak and peek" all you want, but there may come a time you need a little firepower to get the job done—anyway it is something you have to plan on.

The aggresive move into Laos and then bang—one small meeting engagement and "poof," the team turned tail and ran as fast as they could. Supposedly only one man knew where the rendezvous with General Kham Bou was and when he became lost, the mission had to be aborted.

Rangers and Special Forces are taught the basic principle of "double priming," i.e., always put two primers and fuses on demolitions just in case one doesn't go off; always take two radios on patrols; in other words, always have a backup. There should have been more than one Lao who knew the rendezvous. Gritz surely had an idea of the approximate location, and since they had gone that far without firepower, perhaps they should have, as Gritz puts it, "sneaked and peeked" around a little and looked for Kham Bou and Zappone. It was out of character for Gritz to (1) turn tail and run away so easily and, (2) to abandon one of his men to the enemy without making some effort to get him back.

*In late January, 1981, I saw 20 barefoot
American POWs in a camp in Samso, Laos.
They were wearing the letters "TB" on their
backs, TB standing for "Tu Binh" or "Prisoners
of War" in Vietnamese. The Americans were
very thin and their clothing torn. They moved
very slow as if they were sick.*

A Vietnamese refugee interviewed by Gritz

CHAPTER SIXTEEN

3 DECEMBER 1982, 0500 HOURS

An hour after Patterson and Akhein arrived, the dogs started
barking again and in a few minutes Goldman and Boun Thong
joined them. The two Americans shook hands warmly; both had
fears that the other had drowned.

"Did you see anything of Bo?" asked Patterson.

"No. We didn't see anyone," said Goldman, shaking his head. "Is
that really food I see?"

The newcomers sat down and ravenously began stuffing food
into their mouths. After they had sated their appetites, Boun
Thong caught a ride into That Phanom on the back of the farmer's
motor scooter. He returned 30 minutes later with a battered
pickup truck. They all loaded into the truck and headed north.
After two delays caused by the radiator overheating, they finally
arrived at Loh's about 0900. There, they found a tired Bo Gritz
waiting for them. They all sat down together and considered their
good luck at having survived the swim. After all, the Mekong was
supposed to be unswimmable!

Gritz had hitched a ride from his beaching area, which was
several miles downstream from the others, and was taken to That
Phanom where he told the curious authorities that he was an
employee of ESSO and had fallen into the Mekong while doing an
oil survey. He gave them Loh's phone number and the Thai official
phoned the Vietnamese, who confirmed Gritz's story. Apparently

the authorities believed him because they released him without any more questions.

There was a message waiting for them, which had arrived while they were in Laos:

CLINT AND I MET WITH PRESIDENT ON 27TH. PRES-IDENT SAID: QUOTE, IF YOU BRING OUT ONE U.S. POW, I WILL START WORLD WAR III TO GET THE REST OUT. UNQUOTE. GOOD LUCK!

WILSON

"See!" said Bo with enthusiasm, "I told you—all we have to do is get one damned POW and Reagan will send in the U.S. Marines to get us out."

The team rested that day, nursed their wounds and doctored their badly mangled feet. As it turned out, their feet were the least prepared part of their body for the incursion into Laos. Patterson's foot was badly infected and he was running a high fever. He had two cracked ribs and a rash of unknown origin over most of his body. He knew that he would need at least a week to recover before he could go back into Laos. Gritz decided that he couldn't wait a week. Even though both he and Goldman were in poor physical shape, he believed that he had to get back across the river as soon as possible. He feared that if the DIA or CIA found out that he went into Laos and returned, they would put pressure on the Thai Government to shut down the operation. Gritz was also very worried about Zappone. He didn't want the world to know he lost a man trying to free POWs. He had to do something to get Zappone back.

On the 4th, Gritz and Goldman went to the crossing site only to find that a large North Vietnamese and Pathet Lao force was using it, so they were forced to postpone the operation.

They went again the evening of the 5th. This time the crossing master did not return after saying he had to go to Muk Da Han to pick up the weapons for the Free Lao security force.

The next day, Gritz received word from the crossing master that the mission was a "go" for the 9th. The good news included the fact that both Akhein and Boun Thong would be available to return with them. Late that afternoon the team received some startling news about Dominic Zappone. One of Loh's agents walked in from Laos and reported that Zappone was being held captive by people loyal to Phoumi Nosavon and they were willing to ransom him back to the Americans. If this was true, then they had not been ambushed by the Communists—they had been hit by Free Lao forces! It was also possible that Phoumi had gotten his revenge for their deserting him. Patterson couldn't figure out what was going on. He had trusted Akhein completely and the Lao was so damn sure that they had been ambushed by the Communists. There was a mystery here and Patterson couldn't find the answer.

Early on the 9th, the team received a message from Wilson saying he would arrive in Bangkok that night. Gritz called Patterson aside and told him to go to Bangkok and meet with Wilson. Patterson's and Zappone's visas were due to expire in a few days; the other team members' visas would expire in a few weeks, so a trip to Bangkok was necessary anyway.

"I want you to have a long talk with Wilson and find out just whose side he is on. With everything that has happened, I'm beginning to wonder about his loyalty. And remember, Loh's test must be given by an unbiased operator. Don't deal with any of those asshole doorkeepers at the Embassy!"

AUTHOR'S NOTE: Gordon Wilson had been one of the first men Gritz recruited during *Operation Velvet Hammer*. It seems by this time the ex-Green Beret would have been sure of Wilson—one way or the other.

Gritz still planned to go on with the polygraph on Loh. He was convinced that once the President saw that the source of their intelligence was telling the truth, he would support the rescue mission. Loh was a little reluctant to undergo another test. He claimed that when the DIA gave him the last test, they had taken a map and several documents from him and never returned them— then they called him a liar. According to the DIA, it was obvious that Loh was not telling the truth. "When we asked him if his name was Loh Tharaphant, the needle jumped all over the place."

Gritz emphasized to Patterson that he didn't want Wilson to know about Zap's capture. "Just tell him that you were injured and we brought you back as far as the Mekong before continuing with the mission."

Patterson caught the early evening bus to Bangkok. As he was leaving, Gritz and Goldman were putting their rucksacks in the back of Loh's pickup. He suddenly felt a stab of guilt for not being able to go with them. He almost changed his mind at the last minute—but then he realized he would just hold them back.

He rode all night arriving in Bangkok at 0500 the next morning. The all-night ride from NKP to Bangkok was a trip to remember. By the time Patterson climbed out of the bus, every bone in his body had been jarred to the breaking point.

Patterson took a taxi to the Imperial Hotel. The desk clerk informed him that Mr. Wilson was not registered. Patterson only had about 100 Bhat ($4.00) in his pocket—not enough to pay for a room. He went ahead and registered, telling the clerk he would pay his bill when his friend arrived, hoping Wilson would arrive.

At 1000 hours, there was a knock at his door. Patterson opened it to find Gordon Wilson standing there. "Where in the hell have you been?" he asked.

Wilson walked past him and sat in the single leather chair. "I'm staying at the Siam Intercontinental."

This struck Patterson as being a little odd. His room was about $18.00 a day, but at the luxurious Siam Intercontinental rooms cost between $75 and $100 a day. Since the team was running short of money, Wilson should not be staying there. Maybe he's paying for it out of his own pocket, thought Patterson.

"What are you doing back in Thailand?" asked Wilson.

"I ran a stick through my foot and got blood poisoning. Bo brought me back as far as the Mekong where I caught a sampan across. Bo turned around and went back on the mission," lied Patterson.

"Are you sure that's all that's going on?"

"Yes. That's it. Now what about the polygraph operator? Where's he? I need to call Loh and tell him when to come down, or are you going to do it at NKP?"

"I didn't bring an operator."

"What do you mean, you didn't bring one? Bo sent you the money for his ticket."

"We are going to have to use one from the Embassy. Loh will take the test there, tomorrow morning."

Patterson came uncorked. "Gordon, you know gawd-damned well that Bo told you, and he told everybody on the team, we don't work with the DIA people and we don't work with the CIA people! He said stay away from the Embassy. We don't want those fuckers to know what we are doing. They'll just screw up things."

"If we want the President's support, it has to be a government polygraph operator. Otherwise, no chance of support. The President will not take the word of a private operator. And there's nothing else I can do about it."

Patterson sat down on the edge of the bed and thought. He wished he could talk to Bo. Gritz was really going to be pissed. He had been adamant about not working with the Embassy people. However, if Wilson was telling the truth, there might be a chance of getting the President's help, provided Loh passed the test. Since he couldn't consult with Bo, a decision had to be made now.

"Okay. If Loh wants to go for it, fine. If he tells you to fuck off, then that's it. I just hope things go down alright."

"When you call Loh, tell him I'll meet him at twelve o'clock tomorrow in front of the Embassy," said Wilson.

"Okay. Now, I have some questions that Bo wanted me to ask," announced Patterson, changing the topic of conversation.

"What?"

"Well first, whose side are you on?"

"What do you mean? Whose side am I on? What kind of crap are you talking?"

"Why didn't we get the maps for the first 65 miles into Laos?" asked Patterson.

"I told Batchelor about the maps. He was supposed to get them."

"Batchelor claims you never mentioned a thing to him about the maps," Patterson shot back.

"Well, then he's lying!" declared Wilson emphatically.

"What about the hand-cranked generator? We needed that, but you never sent it."

"I was just too damn busy to get the generator. I was trying to line things up with the President. It's not easy to set up a meeting with the President of the United States. I've been working my ass off for this operation."

"Why did you send us fucked up ammunition?"

"I don't know anything about the ammunition—that was Ramon's responsibility; I turned it over to him. Pat, I don't like this bullshit. What's wrong with you and Bo? If I'm not trusted, I might as well leave right now!"

"That's not the idea," returned Patterson. "We just want some straight answers. Now tell me about the meeting with the President. Do you think he's serious about supporting us?"

"Hell, yes! Eastwood and I met with Reagan on the 27th at his ranch near Santa Barbara. The President is very interested in the POW problem. At one time, he got all choked up, and with tears in his eyes he said, 'If you guys can do it and bring me back one prisoner, I'll start World War III to get the rest!' And I believe he would do it!"

That sounded like something Reagan might say! Patterson believed Wilson about the meeting with the President.

They walked into the U.S. Embassy at 1300. Two people met them at the door and greeted Wilson like old "shit house buddies." Patterson knew one of them: Lieutenant Colonel Denny Lane, the DIA attache who had served with Patterson 12 years ago in the 46th Special Forces Company in Thailand. Patterson had a lot of respect for Lane then. He was a fine officer. The other man was introduced as Francis Sherry. He was Mr. CIA at the Embassy.

Sherry attacked Patterson immediately. "What the hell have you guys been doing up north? How many teams do you have out up there?"

Patterson hadn't even had a chance to speak to his old friend. He was shocked—not only by Sherry's unfriendly attitude but also by the fact that he knew what they were doing. "I don't know what you are talking about. I came to the Embassy to have four visas renewed, and I would appreciate some assistance."

"Well, you can't get your visas renewed here!" shot back Sherry.

Denny Lane was more friendly. He reached out and shook Patterson's hand. "It's good to see you again, Pat. Come on down to my office and let's talk."

Once inside Lane's office, the CIA man turned on Patterson and again started a grilling session. He shot questions at Patterson like machine gun bursts: "What are you doing up north? There's another team north of you. What do you know about it? What are you guys doing, stirring up the border?"

Patterson just stared at "Sergeant Friday." His low boiling point was beginning to simmer.

"Are you sure *SOF (Soldier of Fortune Magazine)* doesn't have a team up there stirring up shit?" asked Denny Lane, heatedly.

"I don't know anything about *SOF!*" answered Patterson, truthfully.

Lane turned to the CIA man. "Why don't you leave us alone for a few minutes. Pat and I are old friends." The agent stalked out of the room.

"What's with that guy?" asked Patterson. "He's treating me like I'm the fucking enemy!"

Lane smiled. "Well, we've heard that you and Bo consider us the enemy." He turned serious. "Pat, you were a good soldier, one of the best. Do you have any idea of the kind of mess you're in? You guys are not making friends here."

"We're not doing anything illegal, Denny. We're just doing something that has to be done. Something you guys should have done a long time ago."

"Well, I can't help you get your visas renewed," returned Lane. "By the way, we have been listening to every radio contact you people have made."

Patterson felt an instant of panic. The only way they could have monitored the Team's messages was if they had the codes and frequencies. There was only one way they could get them! Patterson shot a hard look at Wilson. There was no reaction from the smooth ex-CIA man.

Denny Lane continued, "We have been monitoring you for the last week and a half."

Sherry re-entered the office and asked, "Where's Gritz now?"

Patterson had taken all he could from the "wise ass" CIA agent. He turned toward Sherry: "You bastards have sat on this shit for 10 years now, knowing these Americans are there. As far as I'm concerned, every fucking CIA asshole over here ought to back into the pay line, 'cause you sure as hell haven't earned your money! Now you're afraid that we'll rescue a prisoner and the truth will come out that you have been hiding this shit for years. You're afraid we'll show you assholes up for what you are!"

Things were beginning to tense up in the small office. Wilson still hadn't said the first word. The company man looked as if he was going to swing at Patterson. Patterson hoped he would! Lane wished that Sherry had left this meeting up to him; he thought he could handle Patterson. Lane put his hand on Patterson's shoulder. "Calm down, Pat. We're all on the same side. We are doing everything we can to bring a solution to the POW problem. It's just that you independent operators cause us a lot of problems. What about intel? Did you pick up any in Laos?"

"Yes, as a matter of fact, I have a complete *Order of Battle Handbook for Central Laos.* It came off of an NVA lieutenant who doesn't have any need for it any more!"

"Recent?" asked Lane.

"Current!"

"Can I take a look at it?"

Patterson opened his briefcase and handed the booklet to Lane. "Here, you can copy it. But that's the only thing I'm giving you, and I'm only doing that because it pertains to national security."

Denny Lane thumbed through the handbook. It was in Thai, which he could read. "Yes, this is good stuff!" he announced. He pushed a buzzer on his desk and a sergeant walked in. "Here, take this; burn me a copy."

"Where did you get the handbook?" asked Sherry.

"One of our indigenous patrols ambushed an NVA unit."

"Do you understand what violating the Neutrality Act means?"

Patterson exploded, "If you can find twelve honest, red-blooded Americans who would convict us, then we've got it coming. Otherwise—kiss off!"

"You guys are going to buy yourselves a peck of trouble if you don't call it off," warned Sherry. "Tell Gritz to get his ass back into Thailand."

The sergeant returned and gave Lane the handbook, who handed it back to Patterson. "Thanks, Pat. I appreciate your giving me that. What Sherry says is true. Gritz is asking for trouble."

"Thanks for the warning," said Patterson. "And thanks for the help in getting the visas renewed. You can always count on your friendly government to help you." He turned and stomped out of the room. He waited outside the embassy for a full ten minutes before Wilson joined him. There was a lot he wanted to say, but he decided to wait.

"You had better fly to Kuala Lumpur today if you want to get your visas renewed," said Wilson. "Yours expires today. The others have a few weeks yet. There's a flight out at 1500."

"Yeah, you're right. Take me by the hotel and I'll pick up my suitcase."

"You'd better not take that briefcase through customs with all those papers. There are too many sensitive documents. I'll keep it for you until you get back."

I wonder how stupid he thinks I am, thought Patterson. Since he was second-in-command of *Operation Lazarus*, Patterson was the custodian of all the papers and documents generated: intelligence reports, letters, maps, financial vouchers, etc. He found the best way to keep track of them was to carry them with him.

Wilson waited in the lobby while Patterson went up to his room. There he removed those papers he didn't want Wilson or the Embassy to get hold of and hid them. He was positive that everything inside the briefcase would be copied while he was gone.

At the airport, Wilson paid for Patterson's ticket with an American Express Card. Patterson noticed something strange. He wasn't close enough to make out the name on the card, but he could see that it didn't say "Gordon Wilson." Just before he entered the departure lounge, he turned to Gordon. "Remember, Loh is only to be asked questions concerning POWs, him, and his agents. No operational questions, and Bo wants you to be present during the questioning. Don't leave Loh alone in there!"

Patterson left Bangkok on Malaysian Air Lines Flight 83Y for Kuala Lumpur, Malaysia at 1500 hours. He returned the next afternoon at 1300 hours.

Wilson met him at the Imperial Hotel with some startling news: "Loh flunked the polygraph test!"

"I just can't believe that! Loh is not a liar! Why do you think he flunked?"

"Because he wasn't telling the truth!" snapped back Wilson.

Patterson caught the next bus to Nakhon Phanom. When he checked his briefcase, he found that two intel reports and one letter from Wilson to Gritz were missing. Somehow, he could see a day of reckoning ahead for one Gordon Wilson!

AUTHOR'S NOTE: Clint Eastwood did notify President Reagan about Gritz's rescue mission. When the President returned to Washington a few days later, he asked his National Security Council about Gritz and the mission. They informed him they were aware of the former Green Beret colonel's efforts but Gritz was "not somebody with whom we ought to be involved."

According to administration officials, word was passed to Gritz's associates to stop the mission. The Team in Thailand never received the stop request from Washington. All the messages sent to Gritz by Wilson and others declared that the President supported the rescue mission.

A CIA-trained Vietnamese Special Forces paratrooper endured 15 years in North Vietnam prisons and claims to have come into contact with many American POWs. Late in 1978, he and 130 American POWs were transferred to Than Hoa, whereupon they were separated into groups of approximately 30 and farmed out to separate camps to facilitate security. "The American POWs I saw were very thin; they were covered with scabies; there was just skin and bones left on them. They could hardly walk, yet they were forced to carry wood from the forests distant about 500 meters. They often fell down. Sometimes they were beaten by the guards. These things I saw with my own eyes.

Defense Intelligence
Agency Document

CHAPTER SEVENTEEN

NAKHON PHANOM, THAILAND, 12 DECEMBER 1982

Patterson rode the bus all night, arriving in NKP at 0700 the next morning. Lance Trimmer told him that the Team had crossed the river on the 9th, as scheduled, and that so far everything was going well. However, there was no news of Dominic Zappone. Patterson glanced at the radio log. Gritz was sending regular daily situation reports. Trimmer reached over and turned the log over so Patterson couldn't see it.

Loh returned from Bangkok the next day. After the test, he had stayed an extra day to visit his son. Loh said, "The polygraph operator kept asking me questions about Mr. Bo and the operation, and not about my agents or the truth about my intelligence data and sources." Loh shrugged his shoulders. "I cannot tell the truth about the operation—so I lied!"

"What about Mr. Wilson? He was in the room with you?"

"No, he was not in the room. It was only me and the operator."

Patterson was furious. He picked up the phone and dialed Wilson's room at the Siam Intercontinental. When Wilson answered, Patterson asked, "Why didn't you do as you were told?"

"Loh is lying!" returned Wilson. "Those were not the questions asked."

"Were you in the room with Loh while the test was administered?"

"No."

"Shit!" said Patterson and he hung up.

★　　　　★　　　　★

Wilson called on the 15th. "The Embassy called and wanted me to get in touch with Bo and ask him to return to Thailand." (This was the first indication of an official stop-mission request.)

Trimmer relayed the message to Gritz during the next contact. A while later they decoded this message:

WILL NOT RETURN WITHOUT ZAP. AM NOW WITH KHAM BOU. WE ARE SURROUNDED—BUT SENDING PATROL ON TO PHU XUN MOUNTAIN.

For the first time in his life, Patterson began having doubts about Bo Gritz. For some reason he couldn't explain, he did not believe Bo's message. It was too pat! A terribly disloyal thought came to him: Was Bo in Laos, or was he still somewhere in Thailand? He pushed the negative thoughts out of his mind.

The next day, Patterson was back in Bangkok, where he met Wilson for breakfast at the Imperial Hotel.

"Are you sure you're telling me everything?" asked Wilson.

"What do you mean?"

"What's the story on Zappone?"

When Wilson asked that question, it helped to confirm Patterson's suspicions. The only way Wilson could know about Zap was through the radio traffic between Lance and Bo—radio traffic that the DIA/CIA was monitoring out of the Embassy. That meant Wilson was their man!

"You and Bo have been lying to me. What about Zappone being captured?"

Wilson was talking now as if he was the boss. Patterson was going to lie to him. Then he thought better; he realized the situation was changed. The bastards had set them up.

"Zap got captured. Bo is trying to get him back. I really don't know any more than that."

"Was he captured by the Communists?" asked Wilson.

"We thought so at the time, but now I'm not so sure."

"Phoumi Nosavon's people?"

"We heard that some of Phoumi's people may have him."

"How come you didn't tell me that before?" said Wilson, irritably.

"I had my orders. Besides, I didn't know where you stood before, Gordon. I don't know whose side you're on any more. You let us down on the maps. You let us down on the hand-cranked generator. You let us down on the ammo. I'm beginning to think it was on purpose. Loh's lie detector test was supposed to be held at a neutral location, by an unbiased operator; no operational questions were to be asked and you were supposed to be present. Instead, Loh was tested in the Embassy by a government operator, on a government polygraph; and you were not present. He was asked operational questions and he lied to protect the Team, and he flunked the test. Where in hell *does* your loyalty lie? Are you working for us or the CIA?"

Wilson didn't answer. He just sat there with a "shit-eating-grin" on his face.

Patterson continued: "I don't even know who in hell you are because the credit card you pulled out at the airport to pay for my plane ticket didn't have your name on it; at least it wasn't Gordon Wilson. I also know that you had all the material in my briefcase copied while I was in Kuala Lumpur. I'd even bet money you turned it over to Sherry at the Embassy."

That weird look was on Wilson's face—like a kid caught with his hand in the cookie jar. "If that's the way you feel, I'll just back out of the operation."

"Well, that's just the way I feel. You think it over and give me some honest answers, or back out!"

"How does Bo feel about this?"

"Right now, I'm speaking for Bo. Besides, you know how Bo feels about the CIA and DIA."

"Yeah! He's paranoid about them."

"I think he has reason to be," returned Patterson. "They've known about the American POWs in Laos for ten years, and they haven't done a gawd-damned thing about it. Now they're afraid that he might show them up—make them look like the assholes they are!"

★   ★   ★

Once back at his hotel room, Patterson began to take counsel of his fears. He had to tell the rest of the Team about his suspicions of Wilson. Gordon was an admitted ex-CIA agent. Maybe he wasn't "ex." Maybe he was a "plant," and had been all along, put there to spy on them and sabotage the operation. If that was true—and if the CIA wanted the mission to fail—then Bo was in grave danger in Laos. If they were monitoring Bo's radio broadcasts, and Patterson assumed they were, then they could pinpoint his location. Then it would be a simple matter of leaking that information to the wrong people. If the Communists killed Gritz, it would solve a lot of problems for some people and get Bo Gritz out of their hair!

He caught the next bus north. His first stop was Khon Khen, where he filled in Scott Weekly and told him to cut Wilson out of the operation. Weekly agreed that it was the correct thing to do and said he would get a message off to Trimmer in Nakhon Phanom.

"No, I'd rather go up there and tell him in person," Patterson told him. "Better watch your radio transmissions. We now know that we are being monitored."

He traveled all night to Nakhon Phanom where he ran into unexpected problems. Trimmer acted suspicious; he tried to evade questions about Bo and the Team.

"Everything's going all right, isn't it?" asked Patterson.

"Sure. Everything's fine."

"Is Bo still with Kham Bou?"

"Yeah, that's my understanding."

"Any word from the patrol they sent out?"

"No. Nothing yet."

"What about Zap? Any word?"

"No. Nothing yet."

Patterson explained in detail his suspicions concerning Wilson. He ended by saying, "We have to cut him out of the net."

"I won't do that!" said Trimmer, positively. "I don't think it's that big a thing."

"Well, then," came back Patterson, "send a message to Bo. He needs to know about it."

"I can't do it now. I'm on listening silence."

"Well, break radio silence. I think Bo should have this info *now!*"

"I can't break radio silence. I'll tell him next time he contacts me."

"When is the next scheduled contact?" asked Patterson.

"Tomorrow night. I'll tell him then. But you're all wrong about Wilson. He's been in on the operation from the beginning. I really don't think we should worry Bo about it. He has enough to think about right now."

It was obvious to Patterson that there was something very wrong going on here. Trimmer, who was always very friendly to him, was just not the same, and he was a damn poor actor. Instead of cutting Wilson out of the operation, Patterson began to feel as if *he* was the outsider. Were they mad at him because he didn't go on the second crossing? No. Surely not. Everyone understood his physical problems. Besides, Bo hadn't said anything. Hell, thought Patterson, I'd much rather be in there with them than screwing around here, playing counterspy.

He could see that he wasn't getting anywhere with Trimmer, so he caught the bus back to Bangkok. It was on the long trip back that he decided to return to the States. He needed time for his foot to heal, and he should visit his family. Wilson had told him that his father had recently had a heart attack. So he decided he would go back, alert the Team members in the States, get things squared away at home, and then return to Thailand. There wasn't anything he could do here anyway. He figured he could be back in 10 days. He only had $10 in his pocket, but there were prepaid tickets for all Team members waiting at the airport ticket office.

17 DECEMBER 1982

The Thai International Airline 747 leveled off at 38,000 feet and flew eastward across the Pacific. In seat number 73, smoking section, sat Chuck Patterson, former Army Sergeant, Green Beret, police officer, and recent member of *Operation Lazarus*. He was quiet, reflective, and trying to put his confused thoughts in some sort of perspective. Sometime during the last month, everything started turning to shit! It started the night they crossed the Mekong without weapons for the entire patrol. Bo would never have done that in Nam. Then came the ambush, and Zap was captured, and there wasn't a damned thing anyone could do about it. It was clear that Bo was shook up about Zap. Now it seems that it wasn't the Communists who ambushed them, it may have been Free Lao forces! The withdrawal from Laos had been a terrible physical ordeal, especially after he punctured his foot. Then came the visa problem, and the way he was treated at the Embassy. That would always bring a sour taste to his mouth for government officials. And that bastard Wilson! Patterson was convinced that Gordon Wilson was a CIA plant—assigned to the Team to sabotage their mission. Finally, there was Lance Trimmer's negative attitude at Nakhon Phanom. Lance had done everything he could to keep Patterson away from the radios when any traffic came in. Why? What was he hiding? Why hide anything from the Team executive officer? Trimmer had also refused to go along with his decision to cut Wilson out of the net.

Add to those frustrations the news that Wilson had given him during their second meeting, that his father had recently had a heart attack! It was high time that Chuck Patterson got home and tried to put his life back together.

The Thai airliner landed right on schedule at Seattle International Airport. Patterson picked up his luggage and got in the customs line. Suddenly, two uniformed customs agents appeared at his side.

"Sir, would you come with us please?"

Patterson looked puzzled. "What's this all about?"

"Your name is on the computer. You are to be stopped and searched!"

Patterson shrugged his shoulders and followed them into a small room. They strip-searched him and found nothing. Outside, another agent was going through his luggage. The ex-raider decided the best defense was to attack. There was nothing illegal in his luggage, but there were papers in his briefcase that he didn't want the agents to see.

"Hey! There are classified documents in my briefcase!"

The customs agent turned to him. "Are you an agent for the U.S. Government?"

"No. But I assure you that if anything is missing out of that briefcase, or if you confiscate anything, heads will roll!"

Surprisingly, the agent closed the briefcase and waved Patterson on through.

He had figured that the least they would do would be to haul him through the carpet and give him a big time hassle, but they didn't. He was sure that friends at the Embassy had placed his name on the computer. "Thanks, fellows!"

When he reached Los Angeles, he called Bo's wife, Claudia. When she got off work, she picked him up at the airport and took him to her home. There, he explained to Angels West (Claudia and retired Sergeant Major Ramon Rodriguiz) what had happened with Wilson. They mutually decided that it would be best to cut Wilson out of the net until they could talk to Bo.

Patterson went on home to spend Christmas with his family. There, he found things in a turmoil. His father was recovering nicely from his heart attack; however, he was going to have to have open-heart surgery. Patterson's wife, Virginia, was very ill. Unable to continue paying the rent on their home, she and the children had moved in with his parents.

On the day before Christmas, the phone rang. Patterson answered. The voice at the other end said very slowly, "Keep your mouth shut or you are dead!"

He was stunned, then amused, but the more he thought about it, the madder he became. What if Virginia had picked up the phone? He didn't need this kind of shit! He had enough problems. He couldn't figure out who would want to threaten him or why. All the Team members were in Thailand. Besides, there wouldn't be any reason for any of them to threaten him. He dismissed the call as a prank.

Patterson returned to L.A. on the 28th of December. He was

faced at the door by Claudia, who had a worried look on her face. "What's happened between you and Bo?" she asked.

"Nothing! Why do you ask?"

"Bo called while you were gone and he said to cut you out of the intel net!"

"He said what?" Patterson asked sharply.

"He said that you were no longer part of the operation."

Patterson was dumbfounded! Claudia's words cut deep. Bo had ordered him cut out of the net! He shook his head in disbelief. "There must be some mistake! Did you talk to Bo or to Lance?"

"There's no mistake. I talked directly to Bo."

"What about Wilson? What did he say about Wilson?"

She shrugged her shoulders, unable to tell him anything, because he was no longer in.

"I thought Bo was still in Laos."

"No, he's back."

Patterson couldn't figure what was wrong with Bo. He believed that he would be the last man that Bo ever turned against. Something was fishy. Someone got to Bo, maybe Wilson. He felt as if someone had kicked him in the stomach. He just couldn't believe that Bo would do this, but he could see that it would be of no use to talk to Claudia. She was just as puzzled as he; and she was just following orders—Bo's orders. "I don't know what the hell's going on, but I sure can't do any good hanging around here. I'm going back home. Tell Bo I'll talk to him when he gets back."

"I'm sorry, Pat," she said as he was leaving.

"So am I, Claudia. So am I!"

★   ★   ★

The next day, he received his second phone threat. "Keep your mouth shut or you're dead!"

★   ★   ★

Patterson waited by the phone for the call that never came. He waited for a message from Bo, saying that it was all a big mistake, and that he needed his ex-sergeant back. Finally, the former Gritz-commando realized that there wouldn't be a call. Bo had cast him aside. Patterson couldn't have felt worse than if his father had disowned him. What hurt most was that he knew that of all the people in the operation, he was the most loyal to Bo.

Maybe, he thought, he should have expected this. When Donahue had to leave the Team because his wife was sick, Gritz had become furious and acted as if Jim was a traitor. Bo had talked the same way about the men who had quit *Operation Velvet Hammer*. He was so obsessed with the mission that he couldn't believe any one of his men would, or should, put anything else ahead of it. Patterson felt a great loss; it was a hell-of-a-way to lose your best friend!

The American prisoners wore blue short pants and short sleeved shirts. The letters "TB" (prisoners of war) were on the back. They were fed only rice and legumes, no meat. The compound was surrounded by wire and there were 12 Vietnamese guards. The guards were armed with AK-47s. Location Mahxae.

Agent Report
17 November 1981

CHAPTER EIGHTEEN

Gritz returned to the United States in late December. The team was out of funds and he needed to raise money for the next mission and to ransom Zappone. The scuttlebutt was that the people who had Zappone were willing to give him back for $17,500. However, Bo still had not told anyone but the Team members about Zappone's capture.

A few days after Gritz's return, a Litton representative approached him and asked for the return of the IDT boxes. Bo asked Litton to give him $50,000 as a refund for the boxes. Litton refused. Desperate for money, Bo turned to a desperate measure. He took out a classified advertisement in the *Los Angeles Times:*

ELECTRONIC EQUIPMENT
1-DAY-ONLY DISCREET SALE

Book-size V/SIC MOSFET programmable state of the art, high-tech radio telephone, secure communication devices. Alpha numeric graphic display, burst Codek transmission plus program entry devices, cabling and batteries. (213) 784-3513.

The blackmail scheme paid off. Litton forked over $40,000 for the return of the IDT boxes. One box was never returned. It was left on a ridgeline in Central Laos.

On 3 February 1983, an article appeared in the *Los Angeles Times* entitled, "FUNDS FOR RAID: TANGLED WEB OF IN-

TRIGUE," written by Richard E. Meyer and Mark Gladstone. The article told of Gritz's desperate efforts to finance his POW rescue attempts. Extracts from the article follow:

Bo Gritz leaned his motorcycle into the turn and gunned it up to the Little League ballpark. Gene Wilson held on with white knuckles, the tails of his suitcoat flying. It wasn't the way Litton executives usually rode to work, but he and Bo had some secret business to conduct.

It required weaving in and out of Westchester traffic to be certain they were not followed. The motorcycle, Gritz had decided, would be best for that. It was a Sunday afternoon, but the ballpark was perfect—empty and quiet.

In the parking lot, Vinnie Arnone, a Gritz commando, stood beside a beige Mercury Cougar. Nervously, he wet his lips, then wiped them on a sleeve. He had spread bible-sized metal boxes across the trunk of the car.

Gritz eyed Wilson. "Check them," he said, teasing. "Make sure they are real."

Wilson gave him a skittish smile.

The boxes, Gritz said later, were "nuclear fire-plan boxes." Commanders in a nuclear firefight could use them to communicate instantly, and in bursts of scrambled code. One by one, Wilson tried them out. He wrote their serial numbers on a yellow legal pad. When he was satisfied, Wilson climbed back onto the motorcycle, grabbed Gritz's leather jacket and roared off with him.

In the darkness of a parking lot the next night, at the Amfac Hotel a few blocks away, Arnone lifted the boxes out of his trunk and placed them into the trunk of a cream-colored Chevrolet driven by Leo Thorsness, another Litton executive and former Vietnam prisoner of war. In return, Litton gave Gritz what he said was a check for $40,000, enough money to complete his undercover mission.

The clandestine meetings were part of an effort by James G. (Bo) Gritz, 44, a retired Green Beret Lieutenant Colonel, and his men to raise funds to search for U.S. servicemen thought to be held in Southeast Asia.

Gritz said he had accepted $50,000 from Litton Industries, money he suspected had been given to Litton by the U.S. Government. Then, Gritz said, he had used the money to buy 14 of Litton's black boxes.

He had taken the boxes to Southeast Asia to communicate with members of a team he led last November on a futile raid into Laos. The raid had cost the life of one of his anti-Communist Laotian guerrillas. Now, in January, he needed more money to go back. But Litton balked at raising it, he said, so he threatened to sell the boxes, at least half in jest. Litton quickly agreed to buy them back, he said, and he got back most of the $50,000.

On January 14, Gritz took out a classified ad in *The Times* offering the black boxes to the highest bidder in a One-Day-Only Discreet Sale.

"That was just meant to show I'm really serious about it," he said at the time. "I'm not going to sell the damned things to anybody, but I called my

(Litton) guy's secretary, and I said 'Listen, I want you to pass this on to the chairman, will you?' And I read her the ad."

"Well, about 15 minutes later, I got this panicked call from the guy, who said, 'My secretary gave me a very disturbing notice.' "

"And I said, 'Yeah, it's true. You guys are stonewalling me, and I'm serious. I've got to get back over there and finish this thing.' "

Before long, Gritz said that the buy-back arrangement was worked out. "I hate like hell to threaten," Gritz said. "It is extortion. But we've come 2,999 steps and all of a sudden some son-of-a-bitch says we can't go the 3,000th."

Gritz, who returned to Southeast Asia shortly after the black boxes were returned, said he did not believe that operating without them would do his mission irreparable harm.

"It just means we'll have to be on the run a lot more," he said.

AUTHOR'S NOTE: This article would have made even the most hardened clandestine/covert expert sick at his stomach. Apparently, Gritz invited Rick Meyer from *The Times* to "go along" on the Litton exchange. He even expanded the exchange story by talking to Meyer about the mission and the fact that he and his team were going back in. Surely, he realized that the Communists have people who read English, too! Talk about advertising your intentions! At this point, every man and woman with any sense who was in the operation should have bailed out. Gritz seemed to have a "thing" about keeping the media informed concerning his activities and future intentions.

The article also tended to degrade Litton Industries. Gritz "burned his bridges behind him" as far as any future assistance from Litton was concerned.

With the departure of Patterson and the capture of Zappone, Gritz was also faced with personnel problems. He solved this by adding Janet Townley, Lynn Standerwick and Vinnie Arnone to the operational team. Weekly, Trimmer, Goldman and his brother-in-law, Butch Jones, were in Thailand waiting for his return. Gordon Wilson left Thailand the day after Patterson, and evidently was cut out of the net by Gritz.

Gritz and his new crew took off for Thailand to activate *Operation Omega* on 18 January 1983.

AUTHOR'S NOTE: The following was given to *Soldier of Fortune Magazine* by Vinnie Arnone and appeared in an article by Jim Graves, *SOF* Managing Director, and Jim Coyne, Foreign Correspondent, entitled: "Operation Lazarus," Spring Edition 1983:

It was on the flight over that Arnone, who had worked on Gritz's operations for three years and raised $35,000, began to realize something was amiss with Bo.

Through most of the flight, Bo and Standerwick were busy working on paperwork for *Operation Omega.* When the inflight movie came on, Arnone, who didn't have a dime for a phone call, asked for $3 to get a headset to watch "ROCKY III." Arnone relates:

"Bo took out his list and said, 'Do you see headsets listed here?' "

"I said, 'What the hell is that?' "

"He said, 'If it's not here (pointing at the budget notebook), read lips!' "

Later, Arnone, who was concerned about maintaining cover for a mission that included two girls (white women are rare sights in remote Thai cities like Nakhom Phanom), approached Gritz with his reservations.

"I said, 'Bo, it's time you and I had a talk.' "

" 'What do you mean?' replied Gritz."

" 'What I mean is these girls are going to be a liability. We don't need them at all, and they are going to be our downfall, believe me.' "

"It looked like his fucking left eye got glassy. I don't mean drugs, but like he was thinking far off. His face got real pale, almost paralytic, and he said, 'But Vin, they're POW daughters and those little people need Lawrence of Laos!' "

"I said, 'Motherfucker, stop it! Your talk is scaring me. Stop it!' "

"Bo said, 'Huh?' . . . like I woke him up."

"I said, 'I don't need this spooky shit on top of everything else!' "

In Bangkok, Arnone, Gritz and Standerwick were met by Weekly and Townley and transported to the Federal Hotel where Arnone, Weekly, and Townley were to stay for four days. Gritz and Standerwick went up to NKP soon after arrival in Bangkok, but not before Gritz took some of the mission money, and, as a joke, paid $50 for a transvestite to go up to Arnone's room. Arnone, who ran off the "Katoi" quickly, did not appreciate Gritz's blowing $50 on a stupid joke, after having refused to spend $3 for the headset. Arnone, who had been frightened by the "Lawrence of Laos" performance on the plane, became even more worried in Bangkok when what he believes was a "terminate" message came down.

According to Arnone, the message came down from NKP just after they arrived, and he saw it in a log book that was being kept by the girls. The message read, "Need Scott in NKP by 27 January to terminate KS problem."

"I didn't know who KS was," said Arnone. "I got the gist of the message, though. To be quite frank with you, I thought KS might have been me, some kind of code worked out for me. Scott Weekly, two nights before, had threatened to kill me."

As Arnone describes it, he and Weekly were alone in Room 276 of the Federal Hotel and Weekly was telling him how he came to be known as "Doctor Death."

According to Arnone, Scott said, "I've been elected by the Team to have a little talk with you. We want to know what you are doing in Bangkok."

Arnone couldn't comprehend the question. He said, "What do you mean? I'm here because this is my second trip on this mission and it's going to be the end; you know I believe that. And I know after three years, I'm in to the end."

"No, no," Scott said. "We want the real reason. We wouldn't accept that." He went on: "If I find out you're lying to me" . . . and he locked his eyes with mine and went on, "you realize you are a dead man."

Then he said, "Sometimes, situations transcend the law and you have to deal with them. I want you to know that I've already killed a few people in this thing and, if I have to, I'll kill you. If not here, it will be in the States."

"Then about a day later this message came about needing Scott to terminate the TT problem. So it didn't take a lot for me to figure it out. Scott went out to get some pharmaceuticals (to make poison). I saw him with some darts—I'm no expert on these things, but I would say they looked to me like the darts that go in one of those crossbows, the ones that look like a rifle."

Arnone said that about the 25th of January, Gritz had spotted a fat red-bearded white man taking photos of the team from a house across the street from Loh's house, so the team was housebound. Gritz called and told Arnone: "We need you to come up."

Arnone said he went up on the bus to NKP and that by the time he arrived, the red-bearded photographer—whom the team was never able to identify—had departed as mysteriously as he had arrived.

On 26 January, Weekly and a Thai translator known as "Miss Toi" showed up.

Neither was on Arnone's list of favorite people: Weekly because he was there to "terminate the TT problem (and Arnone did not know yet who TT was); and Miss Toi because she was, as Arnone describes her, a "four foot ball of energy and a pain-in-the-ass."

One night back in Bangkok, where Miss Toi lived, Bo had told Arnone to let Miss Toi, who was infatuated with Gritz, sleep in his (Arnone's) room because it was late and the walk to her home was through a dangerous area of the city. "So I joked, 'Well, if I sleep there with Miss Toi, can I get laid?' He said, 'Only if she attacks.'"

"To be honest, I thought she was a hooker. I got in the room and until 5:00 a.m. all I heard was, 'Why Mr. Bo put strange man in room with Miss Toi?' Immediately, I lost interest. Then she tried to pump me for information. Evidently Bo had told her he was divorced and had given her pictures of the kids (he has Chinese kids)."

"So she kept bugging me about how many wives Bo had had . . . and this and that. This went on until 5:00 a.m. in the morning. So finally, I said, 'Miss Toi, sun is up, get the fuck out.'"

Upon arrival in NKP, Weekly went directly upstairs with his pharmaceuticals and Bunsen burner. Arnone said he ascertained from other team members' conversation that Weekly was making poison darts to kill TT.

"Well, the next morning Gritz gets up bright and early and says to me, 'I have a very important mission for you.'"

"I said to myself, 'Here it comes, Vin.'"

"He almost killed me with a stroke. He gave me 500 Bhat and said, 'I want you to go to the River Inn (a hotel bar in NKP) and get Miss Toi.' I said, 'Here's the money back. Fuck it, it ain't worth it, man.' He said, 'No, no. Get Miss Toi, take her to breakfast, and do not come back until after 10 o'clock.'"

Arnone said he went down to get Miss Toi, then sat while she ate her breakfast, which took about five minutes, according to Arnone. "Now we go see Mr. Bo?" asked Miss Toi. He said, "No, you fucking pain-in-the-ass. No."

Arnone said he killed the next two hours walking around with Miss Toi, giving her a few Bhat to keep her occupied with shopping, then returned to the Loh house at 1000 hours.

Later that day, Arnone learned the reason he had to keep Toi away: Gritz and Weekly were "terminating TT." According to Arnone, TT turned out to be a Laotian subordinate of General Kham Bou, whom Gritz had given a large sum of money (Arnone's impression was around $700 to $1,000) for safekeeping when Gritz left in December. When Gritz returned in January, the money was gone.

Arnone said Gritz put TT on the polygraph that morning and TT admitted that he had blown all the money down at the River Inn on wine, women and song.

Loh told Arnone that when the polygraph was over and they had unhooked TT, Gritz was standing there reprimanding him. To the right of the kitchen (where the testing took place) is a small space that is hidden by a ceiling-to-wall curtain.

"Well, Scott Weekly was sitting behind there with an UZI and when Scott pulled back the bolt on the UZI and stuck it through the curtain, TT ran out of the house, out the back door, and over the fence, never to be seen again."

"Loh told me that's true. I don't believe Gritz, but I do believe Loh. So I don't think they killed him—that day."

On 29 January, Gritz met with the crossing master and two Free Lao leaders to lay out plans for the *Operation Omega* crossing, scheduled for 31 January. Later, Arnone said Gritz told him on the 29th that the Pathet Lao were patrolling in strength across the river but that Gritz was still determined to go in to rendezvous with Kham Bou.

Something triggered Gritz into going a day early, on the 30th. According to Arnone, he and Goldman were talking in Loh's front yard after their Sunday dinner, when they heard the phone ring.

When they went in, Bo and Weekly were packing their ruck-sacks. Arnone grabbed Goldman and told him to go upstairs and pack. Zappone had contracted malaria during the previous incursion and could not go on this trip. (Zappone was recovered on 18 January.) Arnone had never planned to go into Laos.

Gritz then rounded up all the team members, Mr. Loh, and Loh's children for a going away ceremony. As part of the ceremony, Gritz presented Loh with a Legion of Merit award.

"Before we left the States, Gritz had photocopied the citations for a number of his awards," explained Arnone, who also said Gritz brought some of his medals over to award people there.

"He presented the Legion of Merit at a very solemn ceremony complete with certificate with Loh's name signed by Creighton Abrams, Commanding Officer of ground forces in Vietnam in 1968, and Richard M. Nixon."

After that, Arnone said all present, including Loh's children, assembled in a circle, crossed arms, held hands and Gritz led them in prayer for the mission.

"Zappone is opposite me and we're looking at each other and saying, 'What the fuck!' "

Arnone said after Gritz, Goldman, Weekly, Standerwick and Townley left in Loh's truck, he and Zappone sat in the yard and looked at each other.

"We couldn't talk for fifteen minutes," said Arnone, implying that the ludicrous ceremony had left them speechless. "Finally, Zap said, 'Vin, I don't know about all this ceremonial shit! If you're going to do a mission, you just do it. You don't need all this prayer and medals.' "

"I said, 'I know.' "

"Zap said, 'I am beginning to think you and I are the only two professionals left in this whole thing.' "

"I said, 'I couldn't agree more. Any moment the midgets and

Equipment prep prior to first crossing Nov 26.

Mission prep — overlay for operation.

Shot of Customs at Bangkok Airport. All radios were confiscated this day.

Radio equipment seized by Thai police at Nakhon Phanom safe house. (A PRC-74 radio, a battery charger and a 220 to 110 volt transformer).

*Bo Gritz talking to the press on the day
he walked into the Nakhon Phanom police station
and turned himself in.*

Thai law prevented Gritz from wearing his uniform in court. The best he could do was have it carried in and hung up behind the defendant's box.

*Loh Tharaphant and Bo Gritz pose outside
the courtroom in Nakhon Phanom. Gritz had his
uniform flown over from the U.S.*

The defendants awaiting trial. Left to right:
Lance Trimmer, Scott Weekly, Gary Goldman,
Gritz and Lynn Standerwick.

*Bo Gritz (right) follows his chief agent
Loh Tharaphant into the courtroom
in Nakhon Phanom, Thailand.*

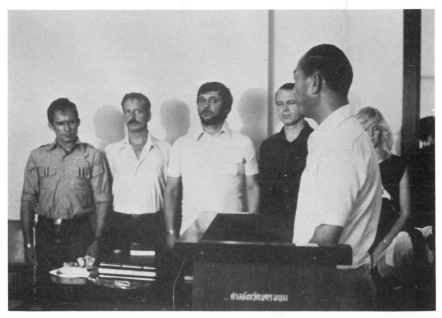

*The verdict was guilty — but the defendants
were given a suspended sentence.*

trained-dog act will come through the front door, followed by Geraldo Rivera.' And we laughed at that."

★   ★   ★

AUTHOR'S NOTE: Every red-blooded American soldier's dream is to have two beautiful girls wave at him as he pushes off to cross the river into enemy territory—just like in the movies. It would also be nice to have a band playing! Unfortunately, it is not realistic nor practical. It is inconceivable that Gritz would have taken the women along to the river-crossing site. By the time he and his team arrived at the river, probably every farmer on both sides of the Mekong knew about the 'round-eye' women, and that the 'farang' Gritz was at it again.

However, there is some controversy about whether or not the Lazarus Omega Team actually crossed the Mekong. According to Thai military authorities, there was no crossing. They say, "The Americans did not cross the Mekong. They hid out in various houses in the Nakhon Phanom area owned by one Loh Tharaphant." The Thai military does not believe there was a 9 December crossing, either. "The Americans hid out in a rock quarry near Nakhom Phanom, owned by Loh Tharaphant."

*I was taken prisoner in June 1975, and was
sent to a reeducation camp in the Ba Vi
mountain area, where five American prisoners
were held in a nearby facility. Every day the
Communists forced those Americans to draw
the plow in place of the water buffaloes in the
ricefields under the eyes of the ARVN officers
who were undergoing reeducation there.*

Former ARVN (Army of The Republic
of Vietnam) soldier, now a refugee.

CHAPTER NINETEEN

In early January 1983, Patterson received the bad news that his
wife was still ill. He hadn't had a paying job in over a year; they
were broke; and they didn't have any medical insurance. His job
prospects were slim. When he'd quit the Sheriff's Department to
go with Gritz, his old boss had made it clear: "Don't expect your
old job back."

After much soul-searching, Patterson made a difficult decision.
He decided to go public with his story. Several factors influenced
his decision: (1) He no longer had confidence in his old friend, Bo
Gritz. The veteran Green Beret hero's judgment and common
sense had been replaced with a driving, uncontrollable obsession.
(2) He needed the money. Gritz had promised Team members
they would receive $500 per week and a job when they returned.
Instead, Patterson was cut out of the operation and never received
any pay. Patterson didn't quit—he had no intention of quitting.
Gritz made that decision. (3) Maybe, just maybe, if he went public
with what he had, he could make the American people realize that
there were American POWs still alive in Southeast Asia and cause
something to be done. He knew that sometimes, to get the government to act, the American people had to get angry! Maybe what
he had to say would anger enough people to get some action.

Patterson didn't believe that going public at this time would
jeopardize the mission nor the Team members. Gritz had kept the

media informed since day one. As recently as a few days ago, Bo had given a lengthy interview to the *Los Angeles Times* in which he not only gave operational details, but also names of individuals who had contributed to the operation. He told about the firefight and the flight from Laos. He lied about Zappone, saying, "One of his men, Dominic Zappone, remained in Laos to maintain contact with friendly forces." Everyone who could read knew exactly what Gritz was up to and how he planned to do it.

Patterson called up Robert Brown, the editor of *Soldier of Fortune Magazine*, and offered to sell his story. Brown sent money for plane fare, and the ex-commando traveled to Boulder, Colorado, the home of *SOF Magazine*.

Brown was interested in his story but he insisted that they "sit on it" until Dominic Zappone was accounted for. He offered to pay Patterson's living expenses until that time. Patterson learned that *SOF* was well-aware of Gritz's activities and, indeed, were already working on a story. On the 2nd of December, *SOF* had received word from their source in Bangkok that: "The U.S. Embassy here had intercepted messages from some Americans in Laos who had been in a firefight. The Americans had left one man behind (presumably captured) and were being pursued by Communist troops." It only took them about three minutes to figure it out—it was Gritz and his team. After investigating, Brown decided "not to print anything until the fate of the captured American was known."

On the 28th of January, *Soldier of Fortune Magazine* informed Patterson that they had received word that Zappone was safely in Thailand. Presumably, the $17,500 ransom had been paid. *SOF* went ahead with its plans to publish the story on *Operation Lazarus* in a special Spring 1983 issue.

Patterson received another threatening call, his third, on 29 January, this time on his unlisted phone which he had installed only three days before. There was what sounded like machine gun fire in the background and the voice said, "You will be dead before the month is out!"

★   ★   ★

On the 31st day of January, a front page story about the rescue mission, complete with pictures, appeared on the front page of the *Bangkok Post*. The *Post* had evidently developed its story independently. With all the information that had already been published, it would not have been a difficult task to put the story together. The *Bangkok Post* is printed in English, primarily for expatriates in Thailand. In the Thai newspapers that came out the same day, articles quoted Thai authorities as saying they were hunting for the Americans involved in the operation.

After a second article appeared in the *Post* on 7 February, Vinnie Arnone saw the handwriting on the wall, bailed out of the operation and headed home. The other Team members in Thailand were not so fortunate. Thai police raided the safehouse at 465-464 Bamroon Muang Road in Nakhon Phanom on the 12th and discovered "spy equipment," including a PRC-74 radio, four gas masks, binoculars, jungle fatigues and scuba equipment. Standerwick and Trimmer were arrested and charged with "illegally possessing a radio transmitter that could interfere or intercept Thai Army communications," a crime that could net them up to five years in a Thai prison. Their "pucker factor" increased by 100 percent.

Lance Trimmer claimed he was in Thailand visiting a friend, and Lynn Standerwick said that she was a representative of an International Boy Scout organization. Both denied knowing anyone named Bo Gritz. Both said they had not noticed the large radio in one room of the house. Loh Tharaphant claimed that he had rented the house to three foreigners who told him they were part of an ESSO exploration team. (Well, why not? The story had worked once before for Bo.) Several days following the arrest, Loh posted a 175,000 Bhat ($8,000) bond for the release of Trimmer and Standerwick.

Meanwhile, Gritz, Goldman, and "Doctor Death" Weekly were supposed to be deep in Central Laos with the guerrilla chief, General Kham Bou. On 20 February, Gritz reached out from the jungle depths and spoke. The *Los Angeles Times* published a story that quoted from a 12-page letter that Gritz allegedly wrote in

Laos on 12 February. The letter was delivered to the *Times* reporter Bob Secter in Bangkok, via a runner from Bo Gritz.

In the letter, Gritz said that another of his Laotian guerrillas had been killed by the Communists. He claimed that he had some "POW ID," but would not report it until he could personally confirm it. According to the retired colonel, he had sent anti-Communist agents to reported prison sites with form letters to fill in and sign for any POWs they could contact. He hinted in the letter that he had CIA-DIA backing. He wrote: "I have 12 CIA-DIA generated targets which, through agent reports and other verification, could hold U.S. POWs. The CIA-DIA knew of our ID, acquisition and test of state-of-the-art secure Alpha-numeric graphic code burst devices, night vision goggles, night vision cameras, etc."

Gritz wrote angrily about Patterson and Robert K. Brown, publisher of *Soldier of Fortune Magazine*. He said bitterly that the story released by *SOF Magazine* jeopardized the mission just as "we were approaching the very target they disclosed."

AUTHOR'S NOTE: Gritz believed that *SOF Magazine* gave the story to the *Bangkok Post*. The *Post* claims they generated the story independently, from their own sources. If Gritz was deep in Laos, as he claims, how did he find out about the story so soon? If he was hiding in Nakhon Phanom and not in Laos, as Thai authorities claimed, he would have had ready access to the paper.

★   ★   ★

On 23 March, an FBI agent paid Patterson a visit. He said that he was investigating an allegation that "Lieutenant Colonel Gritz had forged some letters on the letterhead of the Vice President of the United States, the Secretary of Defense, and the Chairman of the Joint Chiefs of Staff."

Patterson admitted that he knew about the letters; however, he didn't feel that any crime had been committed since there was no monetary gain involved. The letters were just to be used in an emergency to "open a few doors" if the Team got into trouble in Laos. While he was stationed at the Pentagon, Gritz had somehow managed to "appropriate" the letterhead stationery. In Bangkok,

he and his brother-in-law, Butch Jones, went down to the local
IBM office and typed the letters. Butch Jones kept the letters with
him in Bangkok while the Team was in Laos. If the Team got into
trouble, he was to use the letters to try and get help. The letters
said something to the effect that,

"The bearer of this letter, Mr. Walter Jones, is on a special
classified mission for the United States Government. He is
authorized to show this letter only in an extreme emergency.
If you can assist him in any way, please do so. If there is money
involved, the U.S. Government will pay the remuneration
after 1 January 1983."

The agent changed the subject. "We understand that Colonel
Gritz has received some rather large donations from some influential citizens. Do you know who they were and how much they
donated?"

Patterson assumed the FBI man was referring to Eastwood and
Shatner. He thought it best to avoid names. "I wasn't involved in
the fund raising."

"What was the money used for?"

"As far as I know, every cent that was donated was used to pay
for the cost of the operation," returned Patterson.

"Are you aware that Federal law prohibits furnishing money for
any private military expedition or enterprise against any country
with which the United States is at peace?"

Patterson was becoming irritated. It was obvious that the agent
was trying to get him flustered so he would say something incriminating against Bo. "I don't think any court will find us guilty," he
shot back.

"Who handled the money for the Team?" asked the agent.

"Bo and Gordon Wilson."

"Did you know that Gordon Wilson is suspected of taking
money from a fund-raising campaign he was involved with in
Florida?"

This was surprising news to Patterson. "No. I don't know anything about that."

"Do you have any knowledge of either Gritz or Wilson pocket-
ing any of the donated money?"

"No! Of course not," answered Patterson. "I'm positive that Bo never took one damn cent for himself."

The FBI man finally left, and Patterson never heard from him again. It was evident that the FBI was aware of the rift between him and Bo and thought maybe he might give them something incriminating against his former comrade.

★   ★   ★

On 28 February 1983, James "Bo" Gritz walked into the Nakhon Phanom police station and announced, "I'm Bo Gritz. I understand you are looking for me."

Jim Coyne, *SOF* Foreign Correspondent, was present when Gritz surrendered, and later described the scene in his magazine:

"Gritz, who was wearing a red shirt and a POW bracelet with the name Robert Standerwick, was telling them he had just returned from a 'long walk,' but he was clean-shaven and very pale, and his arms weren't scratched. He looked like he had been inside a house for a year."

AUTHOR'S NOTE: Patterson does not believe that Gritz had just returned from Laos—not in the condition described by Coyne.

"You should have seen us when we returned on the 2nd of December. Our arms and faces were scratched, our bodies were covered with insect bites, we had rashes over our bodies, and we hobbled like a bunch of cripples. There is no way that Bo could have just emerged from the jungle!"

Coyne asked Gritz if he still blamed his failure on Bob Brown, and Gritz answered, "I personally think that the names of Chuck Patterson and Bob Brown should be synonymous now with whatever you cannot describe when it comes to loyalty and patriotism; and in Patterson's case, he's a thief, coward, liar, and traitor!"

Coyne identified himself and told Gritz that the *Bangkok Post* developed its own leads for the story.

"You're saying Bob Brown did not release copy to the *Bangkok Post?*"

"I'm saying Bob Brown did not release copy to the *Bangkok Post!*" replied Coyne.

"*Soldier of Fortune* did not?" asked Gritz.

"*Soldier of Fortune* did not," replied Coyne.

"Then I am mistaken," said Gritz.

*If I and my people don't do it, I don't know
anyone in Washington who will. It takes action,
and both Teddy Roosevelt and John Wayne are
dead.*

JAMES "BO" GRITZ

CHAPTER TWENTY

The United States Government immediately denied any involvement with Gritz or his rescue missions and denounced them as counterproductive to official efforts to secure information from the Laotian and Vietnamese Governments about Americans killed or missing in action.

A U.S. Embassy spokesman in Bangkok said, "The U.S. Government is on record concerning how we feel about this sort of thing (private rescue missions). The government doesn't like it nor condone it. We don't support it and it causes problems."

Ann Mills Griffiths, Executive Director of the National League of Families of American Prisoners and Missing in Southeast Asia, was quoted in the *Los Angeles Times* as saying:

"His initial efforts may have been born out of frustration over lack of government activity. However, what he is doing right now is most unhelpful to current efforts of the U.S. Government, to current cooperation between us and Laos. It can only be detrimental to have increased security for the prisoners and to have allegations that the U.S. Government is supporting Laos insurgents."

Fred Travelena, another National League of Families official, was quoted in the same article:

"I think Gritz doesn't realize that what he's doing is counterproductive and endangers these guys (POWs). I am of the absolute opinion that there are hundreds of guys who are over there and at the mercy of some pretty brutal people."

The National League of Families, in its Newsletter of 22 February 1983, stated:

"The League does not support nor encourage such irresponsible private forays which interfere with the legitimate efforts of confirming the existence of POWs as well as government-to-government negotiations to account for the missing. Many increasingly believe that Gritz and his companions are more interested in publicity than in serious efforts to accomplish the goal."

"I'm very apprehensive," said George Brooks, Chairman of the National League of Families. "I believe that men are being held in both Laos and Vietnam. I don't know what the reaction of those governments is going to be. I feel that the relationships that we have encouraged are going to be seriously damaged by this (Gritz) operation, and most importantly, whatever men are still alive over there—I don't know what's going to happen to them."

The celebrated prisoner spent the time waiting for his trial, giving martial arts lessons to the Chief of Police and interviews to the press. He even found time to appear by satellite on "Good Morning America!" The climate between Gritz and his jailers was one of open friendship and a carnival atmosphere prevailed at the police station. Everything appeared as if Gritz was laying the groundwork for his return to America. In interviews, he laid the blame for his failure on the "betrayal" by Patterson, and the publicity leak that he still blamed on *SOF Magazine.* In one article he was quoted as saying, "My critics should either lead, follow, or get the hell out of my way. We're doing it because you don't leave your comrades behind to die in the hands of the enemy." Another interviewer quoted Gritz as saying he would launch another rescue mission when the Thais released him.

Bo was the center of attraction in Nakhon Phanom. Either no one was interested in the stories of Weekly, Goldman, Trimmer, and Standerwick, or they declined to talk. In any case, they began to slip from the scene in Thailand and when they returned to the States after the trial, they passed out of public view altogether. The legendary Green Beret hero filled the center ring, all by himself. It was strictly a one-man "Gritz Show."

The day of the trial finally rolled around. Thai law prevented Gritz from wearing his "Class A" uniform, adorned with his many awards and decorations, so Loh Tharaphant carried it into the courtroom and hung it behind the defendant's box.

Gritz and his associates were found guilty of "illegal possession of high-powered radio equipment" and given suspended sentences. The Thai Government quietly asked the U.S. Government to get Gritz and his people the hell out of Thailand as quickly as possible! With 450,000 Communist troops poised along its border, the last thing Thailand needed was someone like Gritz stirring up trouble.

When he arrived home on 12 March 1983, Gritz was surrounded by an adoring press, eager to hear his every word and quote his every cliche. They had found themselves a new "Sergeant York" to write about; a "Modern Don Quixote," fighting the bureaucratic windmills of government to save his fellow soldiers held by the Communists. It made good copy.

At last the time had come for him to put his case before the American public, and Gritz jumped at the chance. During his first week home he appeared on the NBC "Today Show," CBS "Nightwatch," ABC "20/20," and "Nightline." He also hit the front page of most newspapers in the country. His first appearance was on the "Today Show" on 14 March where he was interviewed by Bryant Gumble. Before the short three-minute interview, "Today" presented a photographic synopsis of Bo's life. Then, after quoting Gritz as having said previously that he had been asked to leave the Army and set up a training camp in Florida, Gumble asked him:

> "HOW HIGH UP CAN WE TRACE PRIOR KNOWLEDGE OF YOUR MISSION? SOME HAVE SAID THE PRESIDENT EVEN KNEW OF YOUR INTENTIONS. TRUE?"

Gritz: "I have never talked to the President, I do have great faith in the administration. Now the liaison did state that were we to access an American prisoner of war, we would have appropriate support to assist us in a successful extraction. I would not have gone forward had I not thought that support was possible."

Gumble: "YOU SAID YOU HAD PROOF OF AT LEAST 10 AMERICANS WHO WERE BEING HELD IN COMMUNIST PRISON CAMPS. WHAT KIND OF PROOF?"

Gritz: "We were there only because we had received a positive signal. If you don't mind me caveating that just a little bit, there were three phases to *Operation Lazarus.* The first phase was to solidify intelligence that we had. The second phase was to evaluate various groups that had said they had the potential to assist us in the liberation of a U.S. prisoner. Phase three was the liberation attempt. We were there because we had received a positive signal; we were there because the indigenous people that were helping us had made the confirmation."

Gumble: "BO, DID YOU BRING BACK ANYTHING OF SUBSTANCE THAT YOU CAN TURN IN TO THE AMERICAN PEOPLE AND SAY, 'HERE'S PROOF THAT THERE ARE AMERICANS STILL IN PRISON THERE'?"

Gritz: "I hope so. As a matter of fact, it was my intent to provide something that no one can hide away in a filing cabinet meaning a POW. Unfortunately, we had some assistance by an untimely press release from a former member of the team and it made it basically impossible to do so with any great chance of success . . . Our agents were given cameras, they were trained the best we can train someone who is not used to technology, and I have made arrangements to have this film processed properly and we'll have to wait and see. I have several photographs of Americans that are supposed to be in captivity, but until we actually produce a live American, there's always going to be the procrastinator, the doubting Thomas. You've got to put your finger in the hole; then he'll believe it."

Gritz appeared later that same day on "Nightwatch," where the interviewer was Karen Stone:

Stone: "WHO FIRST APPROACHED YOU ABOUT THIS MISSION?"

Gritz: "I was approached several years ago about this mission."

Stone: "WHO APPROACHED YOU? WERE THEY FEDERAL AUTHORITIES?"

Gritz: "To quote the Pentagon at a subcommittee intelligence hearing in the Senate, they said that a mid-level career officer of the DIA first invited me to participate in the POW issue through the private sector. So let it stand as that."

Stone: "WHY WOULD THE FEDERAL GOVERNMENT AND THE WHITE HOUSE HOLD YOU AT SUCH A LONG-ARM'S LENGTH?"

Gritz: "What would you do? Send in the First Marine Division? I think the government, and believe me I have no disappointment with the government, they're doing precisely and exactly what they should be doing. Had we been successful, there would have probably been an embrace. But in this case, success depended upon bringing back live Americans."

Stone: "COL. GRITZ, AS YOU'RE AWARE, MANY PEOPLE HAVE GREETED YOUR MISSION AND RETURN WITH A GREAT AMOUNT OF SKEPTICISM. WHY DID YOU UNDERTAKE THIS MISSION?"

Gritz: "I undertook this mission because we received a positive signal that Americans had been located and confirmed in captivity; I took it because, as far as I know, there's no one else to do it. I took it because I was asked to do it four years ago and no one has told me to stop."

Stone: "MIA FAMILIES, AN OFFICIAL ORGANIZATION OF MIA FAMILIES, SAY THAT YOUR MISSION HAS JEOPARDIZED THE LEGITIMATE EFFORTS TO GET WHATEVER REMAINING AMERICANS WHO MAY BE IN SOUTHEAST ASIA OUT ALIVE. HOW DO YOU RESPOND TO THAT?"

Gritz: "First of all, you're not talking about MIA families, you're talking about the Executive Director (Ann Mills Griffiths) of the League of Families, the spokesperson . . . I, in fact, have always worked closely with the League families. In fact, two of the family members were part of my team in the last six months of this effort."

Stone: "YOU SAY YOU PLAN TO GO BACK TO SOUTHEAST ASIA AS SOON AS POSSIBLE. WHY WOULD YOU SAY THAT IF YOU WERE TRYING TO LAUNCH ANOTHER COVERT OPERATION?"

Gritz: "If you have me on record saying that I plan to go back, then I was mistaken. If the government will now do its job, there won't have to be another commando infiltration across into hostile territory to try and free by force American prisoners. The Vietnamese have given us several diplomatic taps on the shoulder. Three days ago the Vietnamese government returned twelve sets of remains. The last time they did that was the last time a rescue attempt took place."

Stone: "COL. GRITZ, YOU'VE SAID THAT YOU'VE TAKEN ABOUT 30 ROLLS OF FILM. WHEN WILL THAT BE PROCESSED AND RELEASED PUBLICLY?"

Gritz: "The film is being processed now. A lot of the film, and let me clarify that, is not what we would call high-value film. I was given one roll of film by an agent that had access to that primary target. I hope that that film will bear evidence of Americans in captivity. You have to understand that the film was Kodak high-tech film. I understand from talking to Kodak people that we used an ASA of 400. They don't know what the quality will be, but I'm going to have that film developed very carefully. Let me say that there are photographs of Americans in captivity. They are on file with the Federal

Government. I intend to release one of those photographs on Monday, Tuesday, or Wednesday, one of those three days this coming week. We're going to meet in the U.S. House of Representatives. Chairman Solarz's East Asia subcommittee that also has oversight of the POW/MIA is holding a hearing, an open hearing, and I will make available at that time a photograph to illustrate that it doesn't make any difference if you have photographs—what are you going to do about it?"

Gritz next went on ABC's "20/20" program on 17 March. Up to now he had sounded pretty good in the interviews. But things began to go bad when he faced Geraldo Rivera, a reporter who had considerable experience in Southeast Asia. Rivera had done his homework:

Rivera: "COL. GRITZ, WE'VE MET BEFORE, WHEN I RETURNED FROM THE TRIP BEHIND THE COMMUNIST LINES IN LAOS. I, OF COURSE, HEARD RUMORS WHILE THERE THAT THERE WERE AMERICAN POWS STILL BEING HELD THERE. WE, AT LEAST, FOUND THESE RUMORS IMPOSSIBLE TO SUBSTANTIATE. THE U.S. GOVERNMENT, THE DEPARTMENT OF DEFENSE AND OTHERS SAY THAT YOU HAVE NO EVIDENCE WHATSOEVER THAT AMERICANS ARE ALIVE HERE. WHAT EVIDENCE DO YOU HAVE?"

Gritz: "As you know this thing didn't start just in November. It began four years ago. Since then, there's been a lot of circumstantial evidence. My mission, beginning this last September in *Operation Lazarus,* was to cut through all the circumstantial evidence, to try to put it on the ground and substantiate it, as you say. The reason that we did launch on *Operation Lazarus* is because we had, in one case, five separate sources reporting eyewitness reports to me, and all of their stories seemed to be accurate enough to indicate that there might be prisoners there."

Rivera: "DO YOU STILL BELIEVE THAT, HAVING COME BACK NOW? ARE THERE STILL TROOPS BEHIND THE LINES?"

Gritz: "Interestingly enough, when I tried to substantiate on the ground the first time, I became a disbeliever. But we responded on phase three of the operation, the actual rescue mission, because we received a positive signal. The evidence that we have today is a little bit like religion. How can you prove God exists? You have to have some belief. . . I don't have a live prisoner of war. And I'm not sure I have a prisoner of war on film. But what I do have is I have a man, and I have several Americans, three of us, who were on the ground, that would describe the same feelings to you."

Rivera: "YOU STILL HAVE NOT CONFIRMED IT, HAVE YOU, BO? FRANKLY SPEAKING, YOU HAVE NO REAL PROOF, DO YOU?"

Gritz: "We have no real proof except like I say, the proof is on the ground there. I think the proof is also in the shadows, in the way Hanoi has responded to the mission. It hasn't been a part of the media, but last Thursday, Hanoi returned 12 sets of remains. I believe it's a diplomatic tap on the shoulder."

Rivera: "DESPITE THE FACT THAT YOU HAVE NO REAL PROOF WHATSOEVER, YOU STILL BELIEVE IN YOUR HEART THAT THERE ARE AMERICANS ALIVE THERE?"

Gritz: "I believe now, I know now, that there are Americans in captivity."

Rivera: "HOW DID YOU GET CLINT EASTWOOD AND WILLIAM SHATNER TO GIVE YOU MONEY?"

Gritz: "William Shatner did give me $10,000; he was buying the rights to war-time experiences. He

didn't realize that I was going to use that
money, which I did, to promote this rescue
attempt. . . Clint Eastwood, as far as I'm
concerned, is a real-life John Wayne and
anything he did do, he did as an American
patriot, and there were never any strings
attached at all. And I'll neither confirm nor deny
what Eastwood's role was because that's his
privilege to do so. I would say that whatever
those two people may have given me would
have been a drop in the bucket compared to the
actual cost of the operation."

AUTHOR'S NOTE: By the time Gritz left Rivera's program, his credibility was beginning to tarnish a bit. He had admitted that he didn't have any real proof of the existence of American POWs in SEA and that the POW issue was "sort of like religion—how do you prove the existence of God? You have to have some faith and it's done on skin feeling and circumstantial evidence."

This was not what the American public was wanting to hear. What they wanted was hard proof (pictures, names, locations) of the existence of American POWs.

We need to decide whether we're going to let those men die in the hands of our enemies or whether we are going to bring them out. I just spent five days in jail and I was ready to come home. By God, I think they're ready too, after ten long years.

JAMES "BO" GRITZ

CHAPTER TWENTY-ONE

WASHINGTON D.C., TUESDAY, 22 MARCH 1983

The hearing room, where the House Subcommittee on Asian and Pacific Affairs was about to give Bo Gritz the opportunity to present the evidence he had obtained in Laos about Americans still being held by the Communists, was packed with press, families of Americans missing in action, and friends of the legendary Green Beret hero.

The committee chairman, Congressman Steven J. Solarz, rapped his gavel twice to bring the hearing to order. A hush fell over the crowd and the large room became quiet, as retired Lieutenant Colonel James "Bo" Gritz stood up and raised his right hand as the oath was administered. He then sat down and began to read his oral testimony:

(1) "Previously, all such evidence of American POWs was of a circumstantial or statistical nature. Now, through our on-the-ground experience, the body of evidence has been nourished to a state of soundness."

(2) "We have located a Free Lao apparatus that can operate within Laos for an extended period, that can escort a search-and-rescue team to target areas, that can aid in the freeing of American POWs, and that can support the safe extraction of POWs from Laotian territory." Gritz was referring to General Kham Bou and his forces. He called Kham Bou "the Simon Bolivar of his country."

(3) Gritz said that there were five independent intelligence sources "who provided positive indications" of a POW presence at one of the targets of his operation. Gritz was referring to the three Free Lao chiefs, Loh's agent, Sri-Kuan, and Phoumi Nosavon (a map furnished by Phoumi Nosavon showed the location of a POW camp) and the target he was referring to was the camp near Sepone.

(4) Gritz said that he believed the Vietnamese had shown their reaction to his activities by releasing American remains.

(5) He claimed the government's attitude was so negative on the POW/MIA issue that it had not even bothered to have him contacted for an intelligence briefing.

Congressman Solarz directed the committee's questioning. He concentrated on three areas: documented evidence of POWs; Gritz's intelligence sources; and the alleged lack of government contact after the raid. When Solarz asked Gritz about the photographs, the Green Beret replied that the roll of film taken by one of Kham Bou's officers had been processed; however, they were of no value because the photos were either just shots of the Laotian countryside or the pictures did not come out because of the light conditions.

Solarz next asked Gritz about his sources. Bo stated that the target was selected based on the testimony of five individuals. He admitted that two of these were known associates of General Phoumi Nosavon—a man even Gritz admitted was not reliable. However, he believed the other three were reliable sources.

When a member of the committee asked Gritz to name the sources, Gritz said he didn't think it would be proper to divulge that information in public. He finally agreed to forward the names to the committee by mail.

Congressman Solarz then addressed Bo's claim of the government's apparent lack of interest in Gritz after his alleged return from Laos: "Were you not, in fact, interviewed by Lieutenant Colonel Paul Mather, head of the Bangkok office of the Joint Casualty Recovery Center while you were in jail in Nakhon Phanom?"

Gritz admitted that he had been interviewed by the officer.

Other Congressmen, some openly hostile, asked Gritz about other issues relating to the operation. He was asked whether he had solicited money, in particular from the families of missing men.

Gritz said that some family members had approached him with contributions and he had not turned them away.

Again, he was asked what proof he had that there were live Americans in Laos.

Gritz answered, "I have the same proof that would be presented by a group of clergymen to prove the existence of God."

When he was dismissed, Gritz came to attention and saluted the committee. It was clear from the look on his face that he realized that he hadn't persuaded the committee that he was right.

So Bo Gritz had his day in court and failed. Patterson cannot understand what happened to the Fort Apache photograph. "I saw it!" swears Patterson. "It does exist! I cannot understand why Bo didn't show it at the hearing. I don't know where it is now, but I did see it!"

Several other witnesses testified before the committee, including Ann Mills Griffiths, Executive Director of the National League of Families; Rear Admiral Allen G. Paulson, Assistant Vice Director for Collection Management, Defense Intelligence Agency; Daniel A. O'Donohue, Deputy Assistant Secretary, Bureau of East Asian and Pacific Affairs, Department of State; and Richard L. Armitage, Deputy Assistant Secretary, East Asian and Pacific Affairs, Department of State.

Richard Armitage said that while Gritz was in jail in Nakhon Phanom, one of his team members gave a sack of bones to the U.S. Embassy in Bangkok, which they had received from the Free Lao. According to Armitage, these were the same set of bones which the U.S. Government had refused to buy a month earlier, and after examination, it was found that the bones were the remains of two different Asians and some of them were animal bones.

Admiral Paulson denied any involvement in *Operation Lazarus*. He stated:

"On the issue of operations by private groups, I would like to make it clear that DIA does not encourage nor support private efforts such as the recently publicized private cross-border venture in Laos in search of MIAs. Concerning LTC Gritz, I have never questioned that he was a brave and capable soldier, and his motives I would question with reluctance; but speaking as an intelligence officer, his methods have been completely baffling to me. The efforts seemed like a parody, a caricature of the clandestine operation, the 'surgical penetration' he purports to be capable of mounting. Considering his reputation as a soldier, his activities have been inexplicable from an intelligence point of view. At the onset, he's confronted with an apparently unsolvable dilemma—a requirement to solicit funds publicly and still keep his intentions private. Beyond this, he's been incapable of surrounding himself with associates who remain loyal to him or the purpose of keeping his intended operations undisclosed. And as a final contradiction in clandestine operations, it seems he always keeps certain members of the media informed of his activities and intentions."

"In the two years I have been closely associated with this issue, I have constantly been kept aware of Lt. Col. Gritz's general activities and intentions from any number of sources. I personally have been sought out by at least five people who say they have been temporarily associated as potential members of Gritz's rescue team and have become disillusioned and openly critical. My people have been approached by even more. I know personally a number of sources who have been solicited for funds and disclosed the purpose of that solicitation to the Agency. I'm aware of many other solicitation efforts. There have been over the past two years innumerable media accounts that have kept anyone interested generally familiar with Lt. Col. Gritz's intentions."

"Among those interested, I'm sure, are the Lao and Vietnamese who subscribe, as I'm also sure, to news-monitoring services. This exposure is incongruent with his stated purpose to conduct undetected operations."

"Then addressing the subject of Gritz's intelligence. Perhaps most questionable of all is the intelligence to which he is reacting. If my understanding of his primary source is correct, and I think it is, that individual has been polygraphed twice by us, in December of last year and eleven months before—in both cases indicating complete deception, including deliberate intent to deceive the U.S. Government. [The Admiral was referring to Loh Tharaphant] This source indicated he has sub-sources. With considerable effort two of these individuals were tracked down. One would not accept a polygraph, but admitted lying, and one denied the information attributed to him."

"I have recently heard Lt. Col. Gritz, on television, attempt to make some correlation between his efforts and the recently announced Vietnamese intent to return information relating to 12 lost Americans. I view this as an unconscionable and self-serving effort to attach himself to the accomplishment of others, achieved entirely independent and in spite of Lt. Col. Gritz. I can perhaps expand on this issue in closed session if you desire, but additional details will not change this basic view: Whatever Lt. Col. Gritz's potential may have been, he has invalidated himself on this issue. Finding brave and capable men in the U.S. Army or elsewhere is not, and never had been, the problem. I think his greatest contribution now would be to turn over to someone in the U.S. Government what information he has, something he has not done; and become occupied in something else other than the POW/MIA issue."

★   ★   ★

By the time the other witnesses were finished testifying, Bo Gritz had been ground into the dust of the hearing room floor—his credibility was gone. He was the man who cried wolf, but couldn't produce the wolf. Bo's admirers, friends and relatives of MIAs, and his once adoring press—all left the room in disgust.

Bo's troubles were just beginning. A rumor began circulating among old Special Forces veterans that Bo had lied about a certain combat action in Vietnam in which he was supposed to have participated.

The saga of how a Sergeant George Hoaglund died was first told by Gritz at a Vietnam Veterans luncheon at the Statler Hotel in Buffalo, New York, on 29 May 1981:

"Typical of relationships forged in battle and tempered with blood and fire is the story of SFC Hoaglund—a soldier who loved life but found that there is that which he loved more. Sgt. Hoaglund was a member of the elite Delta Force Recon, which at the time was the only unit of its kind, responsible to the high command for special operations throughout the whole of Vietnam."

"As Recon Chief and Intel Officer for the Delta Project then under the command of Maj. Charlie Beckwith, it was my job to establish SOPs (standard operating procedures) for every possible contingency. Because these standard procedures could mean life and death, I openly discussed them with the other 26 men in Recon. A question came up about what to do in the likely event one of us was hit and unable to continue while behind enemy lines. With one exception, the group said the wounded member should be left behind in order that the mission and men might survive. I was that dissenter, knowing deeply that we would never leave a buddy."

"Our SOP was soon put to test during an operation in the Ia Drang Valley to locate heavy enemy troop concentrations. As happened all too often, we landed right in the middle of the lion's den. While fleeing to the pickup zone, Sgt. Hoaglund was hit by one of the enemy machine gun bursts that crackled by our ears. He was the tail gunner in our five-man team, covering our rear."

"It was as if we were all hit when Hoaglund went down, his legs shattered. There wasn't even a moment's hesitation. We all crashed back through the heavy jungle to encircle our comrade. Hoaglund was frantic, not from pain or fear, but because he knew, as we did, that to stay meant certain death or capture. We didn't even have time to tourniquet his severed artery."

"The enemy was upon us. Even as we stacked magazines and straightened pins on our remaining grenades, bullets began cutting bark and vines all around us. Still we could hear Hoaglund screaming, 'Get the hell out of here, now!' "

"It was simple; the battlefield is the most honest place on earth. We didn't need to speak; the communication was clear. We all hated the thought of death, but leaving Sgt. Hoaglund to die alone in enemy hands while we ran for our lives was something we couldn't bear. I recall someone muttering, 'knock it off; we're all going down swinging together.' "

"I've relived those few minutes a thousand times since that December 1965, and it makes my heart overflow with emotion. It is a soldier's nightmare to die alone without a comrade's last embrace; yet Hoaglund's unspoken devotion and love for his buddies was stronger than life itself. With a whispered goodbye and a last look at his friends, Hoaglund put his AR-15 to his head and, before any of us could react, pulled the trigger, eliminating in a twitch of his finger the need for us to be there. He had not died alone and yet we had a chance for life."

Gritz told a wonderful tale of human courage, brotherly love, and self-sacrifice that had a profound effect on his audience. He related a scene that would bring tears to the eyes of a movie audience—the only problem was that his story, which was told as the truth, was a lie! However, one thing he said was true: "the battlefield is the most honest place on earth!" This simple truth, known by all blooded veterans, was to return and haunt Bo Gritz.

The Washington Times released the story on 29 March 1983 exposing the Hoaglund saga as told by Gritz two years earlier, as a fabrication of the truth. As it turned out, Gritz was not even present when Sgt. Hoaglund died. The operation on which SFC Hoaglund was killed took place on 29 January 1966 in the An Lo Valley (rather than December 1965 in the Ia Drang Valley). Three teams from the Delta Project, under the command of Major Beckwith, were committed to the operation. Of the 17 men involved, five were killed, three wounded and three became MIA. The only survivor from Hoaglund's team was SGT Chuck Hiner, who says he doesn't even know Gritz. According to SGT Hiner, Hoaglund was hit in the initial burst of fire when they ran into a large Viet Cong force. Sometime during the two hour battle, Hoaglund died. "He wasn't the type to shoot himself!" says Hiner, who received head wounds during the battle.

"Charging" Charlie Beckwith, one of the Vietnam War's most decorated officers, who in later years founded the Army's super secret, counterterrorist unit, the Delta Force, said that Gritz was no longer with the Delta Project when Hoaglund's team was launched into the An Lo. At the time of Hoaglund's death, Gritz was in Tay Ninh, hundreds of kilometers from the An Lo Valley.

After the story was printed in *The Times*, Gritz admitted that he wasn't on the mission. However, he said that he was on a similar patrol and the story was a composite and his purpose in telling the story was to "make a powerful picture of battlefield heroism!" He said he used Hoaglund's name just like one might use Smith or Jones.

AUTHOR'S NOTE: In 1981, Gritz asked Chuck Patterson to back up his (Bo's) version of a similar story to a writer who was doing a book on Gritz. He asked Patterson to lie and say he was on a particular operation. Patterson refused, saying, "Hey, I wasn't there. I can't do that!"

When the Hoaglund story broke in 1983, it was the last straw for many of Gritz's supporters. The Green Beret vets were outraged and the press jumped on Gritz like hungry tigers. Bo found that the media is a lot like a mistress: lie to her and she will turn on you with a vengeance!

Respected figures in the intelligence
community reached personal conclusions that
these reports (live POW sightings) were credible.

PRESIDENT RONALD REAGAN
January 28, 1983

CHAPTER TWENTY-TWO

The Paris Peace Accords of 1972 were not an instrument of peace; instead, they were a vehicle by which America might disengage from a politically inconvenient war. The North Vietnamese realized that America was looking for a way out of Southeast Asia, and from the Communist standpoint, there was no logical or moral compulsion to return all of the U.S. prisoners at once. Thinking that there would be some tough negotiations ahead before the U.S. came across with the $3.25 billion reconstruction aid that President Nixon promised, Hanoi decided to retain some of their best bargaining chips. What greater pawn could the Vietnamese hold to influence America than American flesh and blood? The Vietnamese had already proven that they were masters at predicting American public reaction to specific issues. They knew of the importance America placed on her people resources; therefore, they submitted only a token list of U.S. POWs. Imagine their surprise, when the U.S. accepted the list as final and never called Hanoi's bluff. The Communists could not turn around and admit that they lied and were still holding Americans (that would cause them to "lose face"), so they decided to retain them for future negotiations. These remaining Americans were divided into small groups and "farmed out" to isolated jungle camps throughout Vietnam and Laos.

They retained three categories of Americans. The first of these were the reactionaries. The Communists made a practice of segregating the POWs into two classes: progressive and reactionary. Progressives were those prisoners who abided by the arbitrary rules and regulations made by their Communist captors. If a prisoner refused to cooperate beyond the codes of the Geneva Convention (name, rank and serial number), he was labeled reactionary. By Communist definition, a reactionary is not a prisoner of war; he is a criminal, and therefore not eligible for any of the privileges of the Paris Peace Accords (since they only dealt with POWs). In other words, a reactionary prisoner was not eligible for repatriation because he was not a Prisoner of War—he was a criminal!

The second group was also labeled criminals and not eligible for repatriation because they were captured in Laos and Cambodia. The U.S. had steadfastly denied that U.S. soldiers fought in Cambodia and Laos. This evasion condemned those captured there as criminals and not bona fide American soldiers fighting in a declared war.

The last group of U.S. servicemen retained were those that were maimed and disfigured, either during capture or during interrogation where they were cruelly tortured. When Hanoi staged the popular show for the world called "Operation Homecoming," they didn't want it marred by disfigured and crippled prisoners. (Wouldn't want people to think that Jane Fonda received a snowjob during her visits to Hanoi to give aid, comfort and encouragement to the enemy—after all, she claimed that American POWs were being treated well by her friends, the Communists.)

We know now that the Communists deceived us concerning American remains, so it stands to reason they have been lying to us about live POWs. When they say they know nothing about 2,500 U.S. MIAs, they are lying!

The blame for our present POW/MIA dilemma, and there has been a dilemma since 1973, must fall squarely on the shoulders of those heading the United States Government: Nixon and Kissinger for being more interested in getting out of the war and normalizing relations with Vietnam than they were in demanding a full accounting of our missing men; Carter for writing them off officially—PKIA, Presumed Killed in Action—for his own political reasons.

Our government has never had a clear-cut position on the subject; and it has not given the highest priority to finding the live POWs in Southeast Asia. If it had, ventures such as Bo Gritz's rescue attempt would not have been necessary. Unless the U.S. government resolves the issue soon, he won't be the last.

The rescue attempt by Gritz has affected many people who

have concerned themselves for years with the fate of the POW/ MIAs. He has been severely condemned for his activities, but even some of his harshest critics believe, as he does, that there are still live Americans being held in Southeast Asia. One thing that has never been in dispute is Bo Gritz's personal courage and commitment to the POW/MIA problem. (Oh, he may have occasionally imagined a future movie about Bo Gritz, the greatest American hero since Sgt. York—but what's wrong with that? That's the great American dream!) What has been in dispute is his judgment and his methods. Some of his critics believe that if there were U.S. POWs alive when Gritz made his rescue attempts, then "the Communists would surely have murdered them by now." Gritz still thinks that the Americans are still being kept alive as bargaining chips. "They didn't kill them; they just moved them."

When Gritz retired and commenced his crusade, there is little doubt that he had unofficial government backing. At the very least, he was provided with classified intelligence information and limited financial assistance. His crusade was doomed the day the U.S. Government withdrew its unofficial support. But the government underestimated Bo Gritz. His backers in the intelligence arena, coming to believe that he was "a loose cannon and potentially dangerous," thought that by shutting off Gritz's funds, they would shut him down. However, Gritz believed he had his marching orders; and those orders were to "rescue his fellow soldiers left behind in Communist hands." Resourceful soldier that he is, Gritz simply went to other sources to continue his mission. There is, however, strong evidence that Gritz continued to receive some support and encouragement from several mid-level DIA/CIA agents. If Gritz had been successful in his quest, odds are, certain government agencies would have claimed some of the credit: "Why yes, of course, Colonel Gritz has been working for us from the beginning!" It is those people who helped lead him down the primrose path—then fed him to the lions when he failed. They are as much to blame for his failure and loss of credibility as he— perhaps even more!

The U.S. Government is guilty for the failure of *Operation Lazarus* because certain high-level officials were well aware of Gritz's activities and plans. (Adm. Paulson testifying before the Solarz Committee on 22 March 1983: "I have been constantly kept aware of Lt. Col. Gritz's general activities and intentions.") Yet, the government did nothing to stop him. This no-action stance could have been construed by some (as it was by Gritz and his associates) as tacit approval to go ahead with the mission. Therefore, the U.S. Government is to blame for his failure because key officials knew what he was doing, but they didn't step in and tell him to stop. (Gritz is the type of soldier who would have stopped, if he had been ordered to do so—by the right people.)

Operation Lazarus failed because of several factors, any one of which would have been fatal to the operation. Each one reflects directly back to the lack of official government support. The first, and major, reason for failure was insufficient funds. An operation of the magnitude proposed by Gritz takes millions of dollars. In fact, only a government with the necessary assets at hand, i.e., men, weapons, communications, transportation, contacts with supporting governments, etc., can competently conduct such an operation.

Considering his financial situation, it is amazing that Gritz got as far as he did. There really never was enough money available to make the operation anything but a "shoestring" attempt. Gritz has drawn considerable criticism for soliciting funds, sloppy accounting, and misuse of the monies. His accounting procedures were questionable; however, if there was any misuse of the funds, it was strictly unintentional. No one involved in the operation got rich, least of all Bo Gritz. In fact, in April 1983, he was forced to sell his car to pay the back taxes on his modest California home.

Lazarus was also plagued by poor security. For an operation behind enemy lines to succeed, the intentions must be kept hidden from the enemy. The words covert and clandestine are synonymous with the word secret. A secret is something that is kept hidden from knowledge or view. A clandestine activity is held or conducted in secrecy. Covert stresses the idea of not being seen or declared. The means used to insure that a covert or clandestine operation is kept from public knowledge are called security measures. *Operation Lazarus* did not qualify under any of these definitions.

When Gritz was forced to go to the private sector for funds, he was faced with an insurmountable problem: how to solicit funds publicly and still keep his intentions private. The instant he went public, the operation was no longer secure, secret, clandestine or covert. From that instant on, the mission was compromised. *Operation Lazarus* may be defined as a "public operation" or simply a widely publicized attempt to conduct a secret operation. Bo Gritz was his own worst violator of security, as he always seemed to keep certain members of the press informed concerning his activities and plans.

Operation Lazarus lacked a viable plan. A means of extracting the prisoners once they were rescued is the most important part of a good rescue plan. To get the freed prisoners out of Laos, Gritz would have needed helicopters or STOL (short-take-off-and-landing) aircraft. In all probability, none of the prisoners would have been in good enough physical condition to walk out of Laos. The availability of helicopters and/or STOL aircraft once more implies government support. Also, to get the necessary weapons and equipment into Thailand, Gritz would have to have had at least tacit support of the Thai Government.

Operation Lazarus was launched on questionable intelligence data. Any information coming from Phoumi Nosavon should have been automatically classified as unreliable, since he is a known liar, profiteer, thief and a procurer and seller of misinformation. Loh Tharaphant flunked two polygraph tests, given by the DIA. These tests may have been administered under questionable circumstances; however, the reliability of Loh and his sources still should have been questioned. Gritz may have allowed his personal friendship with Loh to cloud his good judgment.

There was sufficient information concerning American POWs at Sepone to warrant further investigation; however, there was insufficient hard evidence to justify the launching of a full-scale rescue mission of the type Gritz planned. He would have been better off if he had launched a small four man American reconnaissance patrol whose mission would have been to "go to Sepone and verify the intelligence information gathered from Loh and his contacts." This type of mission would have been within the capabilities of the *Lazarus* Team.

If one word were to be used to describe the mental attitude of the principal characters throughout Gritz's crusade, it would be paranoia. Suspicion and distrust prevailed throughout the operations. The CIA and DIA were perceived to be lurking in every dark corner ready to sabotage the mission. Even the President's closest advisors were not to be trusted because, "they would hide the truth from the President." When reputable special operations veterans quit *Operation Velvet Hammer* (for good reasons) they were accused of being CIA plants "sent there to wreck the operation." Later, in Thailand, Jim Donahue had to leave because his wife was ill, and he suddenly became "a traitor and quitter." Next, Jack Bailey fell by the wayside, followed by Gordon Wilson, and finally, even Gritz's right hand, Chuck Patterson. In *Operation Lazarus Omega*, Vinnie Arnone was threatened by Scott Weekly because Gritz suspected him of being with the CIA. It appears that the only people Bo Gritz really trusted were the media—but they finally turned on him, too.

Two questions prevailed throughout *Operation Lazarus:* (1) Was the information provided by Loh Tharaphant reliable? and, (2) Did the Fort Apache photograph exist? There has been some speculation that Loh perpetuated a fraud on Gritz and his associates. Loh was already wealthy by Thai standards and the small amount of money he might have made from the Americans was insignificant. Loh is probably what he appears to be: an avowed anti-Communist with a sincere desire to help his American friends. He was probably fed some false information from his sources, but much of his information was probably accurate. Information is only input—it needs to be checked and verified before it becomes usable intelligence data.

Charles Patterson says the Fort Apache photograph did exist. What happened to it, and why Gritz didn't show it later, is up for speculation. A scenario for consideration follows:

Gritz received the photograph from someone in the DIA, or perhaps from Ann Mills Griffiths, who received it from the DIA. When his contacts withdrew their support during *Operation Grand Eagle,* they took back the classified photo; or when Ann Mills Griffiths and Gritz split up, she took it back and returned it to the DIA. Where is it today? Quite probably buried deep in the DIA's myriad of classified documents pertaining to the POW/MIA issue. If you want something to disappear—classify it!

★   ★   ★

Since 1982, the administration has made some halfhearted efforts to solve the POW/MIA issue. On 28 January 1982, President Reagan, speaking before the National League of POW/MIA Families, stated that, "Respected figures in the intelligence community reached personal conclusions that these reports (live POW sightings) were credible."

This admission by the President of the United States, that the U.S. Government now believed that there were Americans being detained against their will in Laos and Vietnam, should have raised the priority and increased the government's commitment to solve the POW/MIA problem. The government claims that since 1982, all live sightings have been thoroughly investigated and further, "new diplomatic actions have been initiated with the governments of Laos and Vietnam in an attempt to solve the issue." Although no major breakthrough has been made, at least two crash sites have been jointly excavated.

The Grenada invasion proved that the current administration has the resolve to act positively when American lives and interests are in jeopardy. If the President was presented with positive evidence that Americans were being held in Southeast Asia, he would probably do whatever necessary to get them out. If a location was identified, he would no doubt order a rescue mission similar to the Son Tay raid. The question is, *does the United States have the capability to successfully conduct such a mission?*

The 1970 Son Tay raid into North Vietnam, 23 miles from downtown Hanoi, proved abortive. When the 56 American Green Berets landed in the middle of the night, they found the camp empty of POWs. But the mission was well planned and executed, and not one raider was killed. Had the intelligence not been faulty, the raid would have been successful. Since then, the U.S. has improved its capability to conduct these type missions. There are two units that are trained and ready: The Delta Force (the U.S. anti-terrorist group) and the U.S. Army Ranger Battalions. Which unit would be used would depend upon the size and magnitude of the operation.

LTC James G. "Bo" Gritz and *Operation Lazarus* have both faded into history amidst a storm of controversy. His intentions were honorable and his zeal and dedication is to be admired, but his methods were baffling and the results hurt many people. He has forever invalidated himself as a contributor in solving the POW/MIA issue. The issue itself may never be solved. We may never know for sure. However, there is one thing for certain: *if the POWs are there, each day that passes decreases the likelihood of survivors.* And, as time passes, the MIAs are remembered by fewer and fewer people. As Chuck Patterson put it so bluntly "I don't think anyone really gives a shit anymore!"

Did the Communists retain American POWs in Southeast Asia after *Operation Homecoming* in 1973? How can anyone with normal intelligence think otherwise? But that is no longer the question. The question now is *how many are still alive, and what is our government going to do about it?*

"We had been told, on leaving our native soil, that we were going to defend the sacred rights conferred on us by so many of our citizens settled overseas, so many years of our presence, so many benefits brought by us to populations in need of our assistance and our civilization."

"We were able to verify that all this was true, and, because it was true, we did not hesitate to shed our quota of blood, to sacrifice our youth and our hopes. We regretted nothing, but whereas we over here are inspired by this frame of mind, I am told that in Rome factions and conspiracies are rife, that treachery flourishes, and that many people in their uncertainty and confusion lend a ready ear to the dire temptations of relinquishment and vilify our action."

"I cannot believe that all this is true and yet recent wars have shown how pernicious such a state of mind could be and to where it could lead."

"Make haste to reassure me, I beg you, and tell me that our fellow-citizens understand us, support us and protect us as we ourselves are protecting the glory of the Empire."

"If it should be otherwise, if we should have to leave our

bleached bones on these desert sands in vain, then beware of
the anger of the Legions!"

> Marcus Flavinius
> Centurion in the 2nd Cohort of
> the Augusta Legion, to his cousin
> Tertullus in Rome

Robert Garwood says Vietnam didn't return
some American Prisoners of War.

BILL PAUL
December 4, 1984

EPILOGUE

Former Marine PFC Robert Garwood remained in Vietnam long after other Americans left. He stayed because he wanted to. He finally returned to the U.S. in 1979. He was court-martialed and found guilty of "collaboration with the enemy."

The U.S. Government tried to interview Garwood about American POWs when he first returned, but he refused to cooperate. During his court-martial he did not take the stand, and in his 1983 biography, *Conversations With The Enemy*, he never mentioned other POWs.

However, he came forward and talked to Bill Paul, Staff Reporter of the *Wall Street Journal* in late 1984 because he said he wanted to clear his conscience.

Mr. Garwood now says he knows that in the late 1970s Americans still were being held at four places: prison camps at Bat Bat and Yen Bay (35 miles and 80 miles northwest of Hanoi); at a military complex on Ly Nam De Street in Hanoi; and at a warehouse in Gia Lam, a suburb east of Hanoi. He says some American captives at Bat Bat were used as guinea pigs in a course on psychological warfare given by the Vietnamese to visiting Cuban and Palestinian groups.

General Eugene Tighe, who was Director of the Defense Intelligence Agency until he retired in 1981, says that "Garwood's story doesn't sound unrealistic at all. Some of his data coincides with data in the possession of the DIA." General Tighe's former deputy at the DIA, Admiral Jerry Tuttle, says that parts of Garwood's story are consistent with the reports he heard while at the agency. (Both officers were provided with advance copies of Garwood's story.)

Mr. Garwood's psychiatrist, C. Robert Showalter, says that Garwood first told him about remaining POWs six months ago. Dr. Showalter says that Garwood's recollections of his 14 years in

Vietnam have become clearer and more coherent during the past year, and like many other Vietnam veterans, Mr. Garwood is said to suffer "post-traumatic stress disorder," a condition characterized by painful re-experiencing of wartime events in nightmares and in flashbacks.

Garwood says that from 1970 until the fall of 1973, he was held by the Vietnamese at Bat Bat. He was then moved to Gia Lam, where he stayed until 1975. From 1975 to 1979 he was at Yen Bay but he often visited Bat Bat and Giam Lam. He saw American prisoners, he says, at each of those locations, and once he observed a group of them being moved by train. He says he heard the men speak to one another in American-accented English. He says that Vietnamese guards told him about U.S. captives in Vietnam, and they discussed American POWs in his presence. Mr. Garwood, who speaks Vietnamese, says he had a standing order not to talk with other Americans.

Garwood doesn't know many of the prisoners' names. Asked to make a list, he wrote down 10 partial names, including four that appear to be last names. Nevertheless, a check of Garwood's list against the official U.S. MIA list suggests at least a few possible matches.

Mr. Garwood says he knew of 40 to 60 prisoners at Yen Bay, 20 or so at Bat Bat, six at Gia Lam and six or seven at Ly Nam De. The most dramatic sighting, he says, occurred one night in the summer of 1977, when he was sent to fix a truck. He had to wait for a stopped train that was blocking the road near Yen Bay.

It was a long train of boxcars, each one full of prisoners, mostly Vietnamese. "They had them packed so full of people that some had died of suffocation inside these boxcars," Garwood recalls. "The other prisoners were taking the bodies off the boxcars and laying them 10 to 15 feet from the railroad tracks. Suddenly, someone gave the order down the line to open up all the boxcars. I guess to let them breathe. And that's when I saw the Americans."

Garwood remembers seeing 30 to 40 Americans climb down from a boxcar almost directly in front of him. "All of them were speaking English," he says. "They were cursing how hot it was (and uttering obscenities). It was typical American jargon."

Garwood says they were all dressed the same (khaki work

clothes), and they were clean shaven. One man had just one leg and was on crutches; he was helped off the train by his fellows.

In March 1978, Garwood says he was sent to Yen Bay to fix the camp's generator. There, he says, were as many as 60 Americans. He heard them speak English, but was, of course, forbidden to speak to them. "They looked exhausted, but they didn't look starving," he says. "I didn't see any of them working. They were just walking around, wearing blue pajamas."

On his many visits to Gia Lam, Garwood recalls, he often heard the Americans talking among themselves. Once a POW looked at Garwood and sarcastically referred to him as "another (obscenity) Cuban." Not only did Mr. Garwood know these were Americans from the way they talked, but also the guards "bragged" about how they were guarding American prisoners, Garwood says.

While Garwood saw American POWs at Bat Bat the whole time he himself was incarcerated there, he says a significant period was the summer and fall of 1973—after Vietnam had ostensibly returned to the U.S. its American prisoners. Garwood says that although he lived away from the huts other POWs occupied, he often saw them walking through the compound escorted by guards—perhaps 20 or so Americans altogether. In addition, "I would lay on my bamboo bed and hear the guards talking. They were always complaining about how much trouble the American POWs were. Claimed they were very dirty."

After he left Bat Bat, Garwood heard that the prison population there had grown substantially, thanks in part to the addition of American deserters and others who had been picked up in Saigon after the end of the war in 1975. This information dovetails with data received by the DIA.

Garwood stated that some of the POWs were being used for propaganda. He says he was told by three "terrorists" who had been brought to Vietnam—two Palestinians and one Cuban—that American prisoners were used in their training course.

In the fall of 1977, Garwood was admitted to a Hanoi hospital with a stomach ailment. Put in a ward with Cubans, Palestinians and others who had become ill while undergoing guerrilla training, Garwood says he was able to speak with them.

In three separate conversations, Garwood claims these guerrillas-in-training told him that they were first shown a film of Ameri-

215

cans taken when they were captured. Then the commandos saw the same Americans in the flesh in captivity—"like a then and now," Garwood says. "To hear these fellow patients talk," Garwood adds, "Americans were put through an interrogation, like a press conference or something."

After he got out of the hospital, Garwood asked a Lieut. Khoet (a propaganda officer whose tasks included showing films glorifying Russia, Bulgaria and other Communist countries at Vietnam's prison camps) why Vietnam was doing this with the Americans. "The way he put it to me is that the United States tries to build the image that the Americans are indestructible. The Vietnamese are using the American POWs as guinea pigs for the terrorist groups, . . . to show that Americans are only human, that we do suffer duress and stress," Garwood says. He adds that the message the Vietnamese were trying to make to their visitors was, "We did it—so can you."

The U.S. Government's "delicate negotiations" over the years have yielded nothing and the situation remains the same: the Vietnamese continue to lie and deceive; the U.S. Government continues to flounder; the American people continue to be apathetic; the families of the missing continue to grieve and wait. And perhaps in the jungles of Vietnam and Laos, Americans without a country, their strength and hope fading, continue to wait—for what?

Maybe Chuck Patterson was right when he said, "Nobody really gives a shit anymore!"

THE END? (Let us hope not!)

APPENDIX

The following pages provide lists of the names of individuals who fall into at least one of these categories:

- Actual participant in the operation.
- Aware or informed of the operation.
- Allegedly aware or informed of the operation.
- Provided financial support or other type of assistance.
- In some other way involved in the operation.

Operation Velvet Hammer

General Harold Aaron
Eric Anderson
J. D. Bath
Lt. Col. Mark Berent
* Earl Bleacher
Gil Boyne, a hypnotherapist
* Tom Cook
Jim Donahue
* Ann Mills Griffiths; National League of Families
James "Bo" Gritz
Art Harris, *Washington Post* reporter
Lt. Col. Dick Herbert
Harry Holt
Walter "Butch" Jones
Fred Leenhouts
* James Monaghan
* Barbara Newman, ABC reporter
Bob Owens
Karen Page, a psychic
H. Ross Perot
Sgt. Major "Po" Pochinski
Mike Reynolds
Dave Ryder
Colonel Arthur "Bull" Simons
Fred Smith
Terry Smith
* Tom Smith
Bobby Stewart
General Eugene F. Tighe, Jr.

* Sgt. Major Tommy Tomlin
  Gordon Wilson
* Fred Zabitosky
  Dominic Zappone
  Tom Zineroff

* left the operation before its "completion"

Operation Grand Eagle

Vinnie Arnonc
J.D. Bath
Scott Barnes
"Cranston" (Jerry Koenig)
Congressman Robert Dornan
Ben Dunakoskie
James "Bo" Gritz
Harry Holt
Walter "Butch" Jones
Charles "Chuck" Patterson
Admiral Paulson
"Shipman" (Daniel Johnson)
General Vang Pao

Operation Lazarus

* Capt. Akhein
  Vinnie Arnone
  Jack Bailey
  Lt. Ban Thom
  William Batchelor
  Capt. Bou Thet
* Buon Thong
  Jim Donahue
  Clint Eastwood
* Gary Goldman
  Claudia Gritz
* James "Bo" Gritz
  Walter "Butch" Jones
  Capt. Kham An
* General Kham Bou
  Capt. Kham Sing
  Gen. Khong Le
  Phoumano Nosavon

Phoumi Nosavon
Larry Palma
Chuck Patterson
Ramon Rodriguiz
William Shatner
Sri Kuan
Lynn Standerwick
Loh Tharaphant
Janet Townley
Lance Trimmer
Scott Weekly
Gordon Wilson
* Dominic Zappone

* actually entered Laos; "in country"

Operation Lazarus Omega

Vinnie Arnonc
Jack Bailey
William Batchelor
Gary Goldman
Claudia Gritz
James "Bo" Gritz
Walter "Butch" Jones
General Kham Bou
Larry Palma
Ramon Rodriguiz
Lynn Standerwick
Loh Tharaphant
Janet Townley
Lance Trimmer
Scott Weekly
Dominic Zappone

Those whom Bo Gritz approached for help

Capt. Akhein
Lt. Ban Thom
Capt. Bou Thet
Congressman Robert Dornan
Clint Eastwood
Capt. Kham An
Gen. Kham Bou
Capt. Kham Sing
Phoumano Nosavon
Phoumi Nosavon
H. Ross Perot
Dick Salsburg
William Shatner
Fred Smith
Loh Tharaphant
Gen. Vang Pao

ADDENDUM

How *You* Can Help

The National League of Families of American Prisoners and Missing in Southeast Asia recommends that you write letters to members of Congress urging them to speak out and help in making the American people aware of the POW/MIA issue and to support the U.S. Government's current high priority on accounting for missing Americans.

Write to:

        (Name of Representative)
        House of Representatives
        Washington, D.C. 20515

        (Name of Senator)
        U.S. Senate
        Washington, D.C. 20510

You are also encouraged to write to editors of your local paper in order to help draw public attention to the missing men.

In addition, write to Hanoi urging them to cooperate fully with the U.S. Government to account for our POW/MIAs.

Send your letters to:

        SRU Representative to the United Nations
        20 Waterside Plaza
        New York, New York 10010

Further information or assistance is available from the following national organizations:

National League of Families
of American Prisoners and
Missing in Southeast Asia
1608 K Street, N.W.
Washington, D.C. 20006

Project Freedom
P.O. Box 693
Boulder, Colorado 80306

In addition, national and local chapters of the Veterans of Foreign Wars, American Legion, Vietnam Veterans of America, and similar organizations will have information about how you can help.

GLOSSARY

* AN/PRC-74 radios: portable man-pack radios, compatible
  with the V/SIC MOSFETS
* AR-180 rifles: light-weight, silent automatic machine gun
  with a laser light sight; bullet "zeroes" to the laser spot
"Activity": *see* ISA
Army CID: Criminal Investigation Division
Bhat: Vietnamese monetary unit
CIA: Central Intelligence Agency
CID: *see* Army CID
Charlie: slang for Viet Cong
DI: Drill Instructor
DIA: Defense Intelligence Agency
DZ: Drop Zone
farangs: foreigners
"52": number used by American POWs to mark the location
  of their prison camp to identify their presence and
  preclude random bombing by U.S. aircraft
IDT boxes: Indirect Transmission Devices; book-sized secure
  transmitting and receiving devices with a built-in display
  screen
ISA: Intelligence Support Activity
* Inflatoplane: rubber airplane that can be parachuted to the
  earth in a 55-gallon drum
* infrared (redeye) laser-scopes: scope casts a red dot on the
  target; strike of the bullet coincides with the red dot
JCRC: Joint Casualty Resolution Committee
JSOC: Joint Special Operations Command
KIA: Killed in Action
LRRP rations: packets of dehydrated food
LZ: Landing Zone
legs: slang for soldiers who are not airborne qualified
MGF: Mobile Guerrilla Force
MIA: Missing in Action

MP: Military Policeman
Montagnards: mountain people of Laos
NCO: Non-Commissioned Officer
NKP: Nakhon Phanom
NVA: North Vietnamese Army
National League of Families: National League of Families of
  American Prisoners and Missing in Southeast Asia
* night vision goggles: battery powered goggles that can
  increase night vision by 100 percent
OCS: Officer's Candidate School
PKIA: Presumed Killed in Action
POW: Prisoner of War
PT: Physical Training
Pathet Lao: Laotian "Reds" or Communists
* Probe-Eye: an infrared optical system that discriminates
  between human and animal forms and between armed
  and unarmed people in the dark
R & R: Rest and Recuperation Leave
RTT: radio teletype and telephone
"Reds": slang for Communists
SEA: Southeast Asia
SF: U.S. Army Special Forces
SFOB: Special Forces Operating Base
SOF: *Soldier of Fortune* magazine
survival straws: drinking straws with built-in water purifiers
TB: "Tu Binh" or "Prisoners of War" in Vietnamese
tiger suits: special camouflage fatigues
U.S.G.: United States Government
UVVO: United Vietnam Veterans Organization
V/SIC MOSFETS: *see* IDT boxes
WIA: Wounded in Action
"Yard": slang for Montagnard

* special military equipment

INDEX